ALSO BY HELEN THOMAS

Dateline: White House
Front Row at the White House
Thanks for the Memories, Mr. President

WATCHDOGS OF DEMOCRACY?

*The Waning Washington Press Corps
and How It Has Failed the Public*

HELEN THOMAS

SCRIBNER
A LISA DREW BOOK
NEW YORK   LONDON   TORONTO   SYDNEY

A LISA DREW BOOK/SCRIBNER
1230 Avenue of the Americas
New York, NY 10020

Set in Schneidler

Manufactured in the United States of America

10 9 8 7 6 5 4 3 2 1

Library of Congress Cataloging-in-Publication data is available.

ISBN-13 978-0-7432-6781-6
ISBN-10:   0-7432-6781-8

For information about special discounts for bulk purchases, please contact Simon &
Schuster Special Sales at 1-800-456-6798 or business@simonandschuster.com.

To those who suffered and died
for cherishing freedom of the press

CONTENTS

ACKNOWLEDGMENTS

I am indebted to so many friends and colleagues in the newspaper business for their help and encouragement in writing this book.

I owe special words of gratitude to Diane Nine, my agent, who also has a law degree and contributed to the chapters dealing with the First Amendment and the need for reporters to have a federal shield law.

I am eternally indebted to Margaret Kilgore, my close friend from our days together at United Press International, who was a great editor and contributor to this book. She added so much from her own experience, including her stint as a correspondent covering the Vietnam War and as a reporter for the *Los Angeles Times*.

I could not have produced this book without the team effort by "Maggie" Kilgore and Diane Nine.

Lisa Drew, my editor at Scribner, was a great help in keeping me focused and guiding me to the finish line.

I am grateful to my colleagues, most of whom have shared my half century in journalism, who told me their stories, anecdotes, gripes, and genuine concerns. Their recollections are lively and insightful, what we call war stories. We have been eyewitnesses to history, and it has been a great vision. I find that what distinguishes them is that they love their work unconditionally.

Acknowledgments

I want to thank Charles "Chuck" Lewis, Hearst Newspapers Washington Bureau chief and my boss, for his understanding and encouragement, and telling me the book should be "edgy."

I also want to thank Gwen Gibson, another newspaper-woman who served with me at the UPI and later joined the *New York Daily News*. Her early research on the book was invaluable to me. Another researcher was Sue Menditto, a whiz at finding important items on the Internet.

So many more journalists were the inspiration for my assessment of the press corps in 2005. There is Paul McMasters, head of the Freedom Forum, who burst with new observations on the state of the American press. I picked the brains of Ron Cohen, former bureau chief of UPI and an editor at *USA Today*. I also am grateful to my former White House colleagues Alvin Spivak and Ira Allen, and to Paul Mann, an expert reporter in defense matters.

ABC-TV's Sam Donaldson, Saul Friedman of Knight Ridder, and Ben Bradlee, former executive editor of the *Washington Post,* helped me to understand the new trends we face in the communications field.

Others from UPI were ever so helpful: Pat Sloyan, formerly with *Newsday,* and Joe Galloway, a columnist with Knight Ridder, both of whom formerly worked at UPI. And Edith Lederer, UN Bureau chief for Associated Press.

I was delighted to interview Tom Johnson, who rose to the top of the profession in both print and cable television before retiring from CNN, and NPR's Dan Schorr, as well as Michael Hedges of the *Houston Chronicle*.

I also gained a good perspective on media trends from Merrill Hartson, a veteran correspondent and editor with Associated Press.

Others who helped were Kristin Collie of Hearst Newspapers, and Clare Finly, an assistant to Ms. Nine. Dr. Suzanne Condray, professor of journalism at Denison University, gave me a good insight into the dedication of young journalists today. Paula

McKenzie, a journalism professor and whiz on the computer, found some relevant nuggets on the Internet. I also appreciate the help of Pulitzer Prize winner, Associated Press photographer Ron Edmonds.

I am deeply grateful to my nephews Eddie Geha and Steven Geha, who perused the Internet to find information for me on freedom of the press and the standing of the media in the latest polls.

As always, my great family—my brother, Mate Thomas; my sisters, Isabelle Thomas, Josephine Geha, and Barbara Isaac; and my many nieces and nephews, including Terri DeLeon, Judy Jenkins, Janet Grigg, and Joanne Swanson—gave me moral support.

It really boils down to being lucky to have a great family and so many good friends and colleagues in the profession, and I am a part of all I have met.

FOREWORD
WATCHDOGS OF DEMOCRACY

Journalism is a magnificent obsession to those who practice it, including me.

I have been privileged to cover nine United States presidents, sometimes with sympathy, sometimes with outrage, but most often with critical eyes and a conviction that they all could have done better for the country.

Now I have to say the same thing about the press, or what is sweepingly called the media. Something vital has been lost—or have American journalists forgotten that their role is to follow the truth, without fear or favor, wherever it leads them? The truth, rather than an agenda, should be the goal of a free press.

It's not nostalgia, but true concern that makes me believe that the profession had its golden age in the twentieth century—and we didn't even realize it!

Journalists, as the purveyors of information, are the watchdogs of democracy. Without an informed people, there can be no democracy. It is the job of reporters and editors to ask the tough questions of those in power and to act on the answers with trust, integrity, and honesty guiding their judgment. These ethical tenets have never changed, but journalism has changed over time—most would say not necessarily for the better.

Technology has transformed communications and made

radio and television dominant over print in the transmission of news. The technology that brings instant coverage into the living room has also brought into journalism unqualified people who have adopted the modus operandi of true journalists, blurring the profound differences between news professionals and entertainers.

Talk show hosts, many of them on the far right politically, are viewed as journalists. Hardly. A journalist is detached, and the story is the thing, not the daily harangue of "talking heads." With the exception of serious documentaries, there is no way a TV news snippet of half a minute can match an in-depth newspaper account.

Technology has revolutionized the way news is gathered: tape recorders, cell phones, digital cameras, satellite transmitters, and the Internet mean that everyone is wired and on camera. There is no place to hide for officials who dissemble. If they lie, they get instant playback. But something has been lost in the translation from print to quick sound bites and an emphasis on entertainment passing as news.

There also is the growing influence of corporations that have acquired media outlets and attempted to control the newsroom. The bottom line has become preeminent in all forms of media here and abroad.

In the modern age, media mergers, ownership by nonmedia companies, bottom-line management, entertainment passing as news, and twenty-four-hour news cycles have corrupted what we once knew as the "newspaper business."

With the diminishing of print journalism to one-newspaper towns and a virtual Associated Press monopoly in the U.S. wire-service field, the spotlight is on broadcasters and electronic communication, including the Internet, of course, where everyone can offer an opinion.

Unfortunately, media credibility is under attack from the government, political and religious groups, and many segments of the public perhaps as never before. And yet, those same critics and the public in general have access to more news and are better informed than at any other time in American history. Public officials want us when they need us.

Tom Rosenstiel of the Project for Excellence in Journalism said in a recent report that "Americans think journalists are sloppier, less professional, less caring, more biased, less honest about their mistakes, and generally more harmful to democracy than they did in the eighties."

If that is not enough to give one pause, there is management and manipulation of the news by government and a supine press that has displayed an incredible lack of courage in the last few years. I think the media let the country down in failing to adhere to its gold standard—the search for truth.

And don't think the public is unaware of the strange new shortcomings of journalists today—or is it their bosses?—who are too often bowing to government censorship, forgetting the role of a free, unfettered press. I have been amazed at the acuity of the public in confronting and chiding reporters for not asking the obvious important questions at televised White House briefings.

But then, one has to wonder how much General Electric (NBC), Viacom (CBS), and Disney (ABC) care about freedom of the press when access to the White House is at stake, or when they risk losing advertisers for airing provocative viewpoints.

Without a free press, there can be no democracy. It is indispensable to the society that the Founding Fathers bequeathed to us. But do these corporate entities understand—or care about—their public service role?

Remember the political furor over *The Reagans,* CBS's movie project in October 2003? Conservatives were incensed and threatened a boycott over early glimpses of the less than 100 percent laudatory portrayal of the late former president Reagan and his wife, Nancy. The network eventually dropped plans to broadcast the movie in prime time, sending it to Showtime, a cable subsidiary with many fewer potential viewers than CBS. Never underestimate the power of political pressure.

Daniel Schorr, a veteran broadcaster formerly with CBS-TV and CNN and now with National Public Radio, put it best, saying, "The important thing is that the one who sits at the top who decides how much money you can spend on what doesn't really give a damn about journalism. He is worried about the profit line. And it is this palpable concentration of media that changes its character. As a result of that, you get more gossip, more sex, and more violence. All these things appeal to people. They entertain and build up your audience. . . .

"In the end, it's all about money," Schorr added—and ratings.

But it was not always so with the major networks. Once upon a time, outstanding news coverage counted with the big bosses more than money.

Schorr said that correspondents from around the world would come back to the United States every year and have lunch with CBS chairman William S. Paley, who is credited with building the Columbia Broadcasting System into what was called the Cadillac or Tiffany of networks.

The correspondents asked Paley, "Are you worried about the trouble you will get into if you run controversial documentaries? Won't that affect your bottom line?"

To which Paley replied, "You get the story and let *me* worry about the bottom line."

In another version, Paley said comedian Jack Benny would bring in the money. Gone are the days.

Paley sweated out Edward R. Murrow's devastating documentaries on Senator Joseph McCarthy, who conducted a reign of terror against leftists, but later, Paley bowed to pressure and also had Murrow interview celebrities on *Person to Person,* which was much less controversial.

There were extreme examples of government intimidation of the media to keep them "on message" after the 9/11 terrorist attacks on the World Trade Center in New York and the Pentagon in Washington. To criticize the government's failings was considered by many to be un-American in the face of conflict.

The most spectacular examples were telephone calls to the network and cable companies by Secretary of State Colin Powell and National Security Adviser Condoleezza Rice warning them not to broadcast postattack tapes of Osama bin Laden because he might be giving coded messages to sleeper cells. In my opinion, Powell and Rice overstepped the line and abused their official roles.

The networks meekly complied with the government's intimidation. That's a far cry from the way most of the independent editors and publishers would have reacted to such bullying tactics pre-9/11.

I can't count how many times I have recently been asked, "What has happened to the press?"

Sad to say, it has defaulted on its watchdog role in so many ways. The profession has also been badly tarnished by a few "bad apples" seeking fame and fortune at the expense of their colleagues and giving new meaning to the term *poor judgment*. Celebrity status might be the lure for some, but, on balance, I believe young, aspiring journalists believe in the ideals of the profession.

Syndicated columnist David S. Broder of the *Washington Post*, in a 2004 column written shortly before the November presidential election, noted that the editors of two respected national newspapers, the *New York Times* and *USA Today*, were forced to resign because their organizations were duped by lying staff reporters, who fabricated some stories and plagiarized others.

The result has been a housecleaning of reporters and editors nationwide, which no doubt was necessary, but the action has created sagging morale and fear among competent journalists who were left to pick up the pieces.

Broder said it is "hard to overcome the sense that the professional practices and code of responsibility have suffered a body blow."

When it was vital for the press to take a hard look at the horrific provisions of the Patriot Act, it failed to do so. There were few early reports on the deprivation of legal rights of prisoners of war from Afghanistan and Iraq under the guarantees of the Geneva Convention. Only when photographs of the sadistic abuse of prisoners at Abu Ghraib, the prison near Baghdad, came to light did the press wake up and the public protest. But not enough. Not enough for President Bush-2 to pledge that the prisoners of war and detainees would be treated humanely and the interrogators would abide by rules against torture during questioning.

One brief, shining moment in the media performance was when the Detroit newspapers in 2002 sued the Justice Department to obtain open coverage of the deportation hearings of Arab detainees . . . and won. Federal Judge Damon Keith in Detroit commented, "Democracy dies behind closed doors."

I feel that the press defaulted, particularly during the second Bush administration's post-9/11 barrage of government message manipulation and control, by failing to fight the secrecy imposed by the White House. It failed to protect the people's right to know.

In other words, the correspondents succumbed to the "fear card" played by the administration and lacked the courage or ability to penetrate the fiction and falsehoods peddled to them at daily White House briefings.

As Tom Blanton, executive director of the National Security Archive, put it, "Almost none of these White House moves for secrecy have been because of national security or to fight terrorism. It's more of a reflexive, ideological response for more secrecy."

The publishers and broadcast hierarchy also failed to protest the Pentagon's refusal to allow photographs of the flag-draped coffins of dead soldiers arriving at Dover Air Force Base in Delaware, the first stop in the United States on their return from Iraq. The point is that news organizations should have staked out the gate at Dover and counted incoming troop planes. That would have been the kind of wire-service reporting we used to do at the White House.

The executives also accepted at face value the Pentagon charade that it had no accurate count of the number of Iraqis killed in the conquest and occupation of their country.

Nor was there any loud protest from the American broadcasters or other media on the barring of Aljazeera reporters from covering Iraq. In other days and other wars, I do believe there was a greater sensibility and concern when press coverage was deliberately banned for political or security reasons.

Paul McMasters of the Freedom Forum, a journalism think tank, said, "Information is as lethal as bullets or bombs."

Too many times, the major publications have caved out of fear of government reprisals. McMasters wonders at the "malaise of the press" phenomenon in letting the White House call the tune with its message of the day. This ploy was so successful that the Pentagon and other federal agencies followed suit. With the bureaucracy falling in line, reporters were at the mercy of the administration in power and became powerless and a part of pack journalism.

As Bill Moyers, one of the century's finest broadcasters, put it, "The greatest moments in the history of the press came not when journalists made common cause with the state, but when they stood fearlessly independent of it." Unfortunately, too many journalists believe their capitulation to power is necessary to gain access to top officials.

The first American newspaper was started in 1690 by one Benjamin Harris. He said he started the three-page publication "to cure the spirit of lying much among us." The government shut it down after one issue.

From the beginning of American history, journalism has played a pivotal role in democracy as the nation has progressed and developed. The First Amendment to the Constitution, adopted in 1791, states:

"Congress shall make no law respecting an establishment of religion, or prohibiting the free exercise thereof; or abridging the freedom of speech, or of the press; or the right of the people peaceably to assemble, and to petition the government for a redress of grievances."

I am inspired by one of the nation's earliest journalists, John Peter Zenger, who owned a printing press, the sine qua non of a free press. He was imprisoned for criticizing the colonial governor of New York. The jury ignored the charge of "seditious libel" against him. Zenger's lawyer won the case with a closing appeal when he said, "The laws of our country have given us a right . . . the liberty both of exposing and opposing arbitrary power . . . by speaking and writing the truth."

It seems that correspondents in the past were more in thrall to the ideal that set reporters apart from others in society. They were the self-appointed protectors of democracy, keepers of the flame that is the Bill of Rights and particularly the First Amendment.

And what is a journalist without energy, enthusiasm, and integrity, plus insatiable curiosity and courage?

Among the most enjoyable moments I had while researching this book were in compiling a chapter on the early lives of distinguished American journalists of the twentieth century, some of whom I was privileged to know. I even married one of them.

A few among the legion of great reporters from that era include Ernie Pyle, Scripps Howard's great World War II correspondent; Merriman Smith, United Press International's Pulitzer Prize winner who personified the White House reporter; Douglas Cornell of Associated Press, my husband and an icon in wire-service wrap-up story writing; Martha Gellhorn, who covered wars dating back to the Spanish Civil War; Dorothy Thompson, the distinguished political and foreign correspondent; and Marguerite Higgins, who made her name when she flew to Korea with General Douglas MacArthur at the start of the Korean War; Edward R. Murrow, who broadcast from London during the German "Blitz" of World War II; publisher I. F. Stone; columnists Walter Lippmann, James Reston, investigative journalist Jack Anderson, and so many others.

It will be interesting to see who—if anyone—will emerge as journalism "stars" from the current conflicts in Iraq, Afghanistan, and the Middle East. AP's Peter Arnett, Hedrick Smith of the *New York Times,* and David Halberstam of the *Times* were standouts in the Vietnam War.

Judea Pearl, father of slain journalist Daniel Pearl, said, "Journalists, by their very nature, represent the ultimate strength of an open society as well as its ultimate vulnerability."

I have often had the opportunity to question the most powerful public servant in the country, the president of the United States. I admit I have approached the task with awe for the office, but not reverence for the men who've held it. For one thing, I don't believe it is our duty to worship at the shrine of any leader, but to keep the spotlight on them constantly to see whether they are upholding the public trust. Presidents take an oath on a Bible to "preserve, protect, and defend" the U.S. Constitution, and they should be tested and graded at every turn. They owe their positions and their salaries to the American people and must be accountable to them at all times. The media is the go-between, a transmission belt to disseminate facts, figures, and policies to a waiting public, explaining what the news means to their readers, viewers, and listeners.

What makes the press so indispensable in a democracy is that it is the only institution in our society that can question the president, or other public officials, regularly. Challenging a public leader is not required in the Constitution, but if a leader is unchallenged, he can rule by executive order, edict, or act on his own whim in secrecy. Fortunately, we do not have a king or a dictator with unlimited, unquestioned power. There is a governmental system of checks and balances in place among the executive, legislative, and judicial branches, but beyond those, a free society depends on the press to keep the government honest.

Thomas Jefferson said it best: "Eternal vigilance is the price of liberty."

As communications evolve, we have to ask, Why is a free press important? Are we losing the sense of what the First Amendment was meant to be? Is the media failing its constituency—the public? Is the First Amendment seriously threatened?

In this book, I have sought the views of well-known journalists and presidential press secretaries, some active and some retired, on how they view all branches of the media—what journalism is today; what it was yesterday; and what it might be in the future.

I do not think that journalism is a dying art. If anything, I believe it is more important than ever, and journalists worldwide are adapting to our modus operandi—to make public officials accountable to the people. The role of the journalist is indispensable, and as reviled as reporters may intermittently be, they are still highly respected when they pursue the truth and obtain positive results.

It is my hope that future journalists will adhere to the true principles of the profession and understand that they play a vital role in helping to keep democracy and the exchange of free ideas alive at home and abroad.

Reporters should be free to operate independently and be courageous enough to keep a critical eye on those in power who fail to act in the interests of the nation. The media do not—and should not—expect to win popularity contests. But they will be respected only if they remain true to the ideals of the profession. They must be detached. But they must also care.

Most of them know it is not merely a job . . . it is a way of life!

Helen Thomas
Washington, D.C.
October 2005

WATCHDOGS OF DEMOCRACY?

CHAPTER 1

JOURNALISM—A MOST
HONORABLE PROFESSION

While I put journalism on a pedestal as a most honorable profession, I am not saying that it has been above reproach in practice. Too many times the public has been subjected to ethical breaches by reporters and broadcasters that have tarnished our escutcheon and diminished our credibility.

How many times have you been in a conversation with someone about the news of the day when the person concludes, "But you can't believe what you read in the newspapers or on TV"?

Why not? More information is available to the worldwide public than ever before with the proliferation of the Internet, cable and network television, radio, newspapers, magazines, and books. Certainly there is a blurring on TV between news and entertainment, but listeners have a choice to accept or reject what they hear or see.

In its annual report on American journalism, 2004, the Project for Excellence in Journalism notes, "Print, uniquely, has the potential to tell people what they can trust and not trust in an age that the journalist and educator Michael Janeway has called one of 'fact promiscuity, fact chaos.' Or what Vartan Gregorian, the president of the Carnegie Corporation, has called a time when information is in oversupply, but knowledge in undersupply."

It is sad, therefore, to have to acknowledge that ethics—the simple difference between right and wrong—is the foremost internal problem facing journalism and other businesses today. The executives of major companies, including media firms, have established written standards for their employees to follow, but those guidelines work only when integrity emanates from the top of the ladder, from the bosses.

Ethics are something that should have been learned at mother's knee or at least when interacting with others in grade school. An unethical person is not necessarily doing something illegal, but his actions defy professional or social norms.

The National Society of Professional Journalists organizes practical journalism ethics into three main principles: report truthfully, act respectfully, and minimize harm. And, American academics and government advisers have worked with young journalists in emerging democracies in recent years to teach them to be as "ethical" as U.S. journalists in their coverage of the news.

But, suddenly, in about 2003, it became like the old bromide "Don't do as I do; do as I say." With twenty-four-hour TV and radio news channels beamed around the world by satellite and the proliferation of Internet sources telling of U.S. media and business scandals, it was becoming increasingly difficult to argue that American media were a paragon of virtue and respect. The outrages committed by a few correspondents who betrayed the trust of their publishers and the public also weighed heavily against the thousands of honest, hardworking men and women who viewed journalism as a noble profession of the highest quality.

Jayson Blair's serial falsehoods and the subsequent *New York Times* management shake-up; *USA Today*'s Jack Kelley's fraudulent overseas coverage; CBS's list of flawed reports over several months—all weighed negatively in the equation.

To the credit of the above media companies, most moved quickly to fire the perpetrators and offer mea culpas for the transgressions of their employees, as well as those journalist colleagues and editors who didn't question or challenge the guilty reporters. In these instances and others that followed, the publishers, top editors, and deskmen who read copy should have shared the blame for the miscreants' activities and missteps. Many passed the buck.

The media companies set up investigative commissions and impartial "ombudsmen" to see that similar situations wouldn't reoccur—kind of like locking the barn door after the horses had escaped—but necessary to right the wrongs.

There were other scandals within the profession in the new century resulting in job loss—and they didn't all occur in Washington or New York. The *Chicago Tribune* fired a reporter for attributing a quote to a nonexistent psychiatrist; the *Macon Telegraph* in Georgia fired a reporter for repeated plagiarism; the two top editors of Florida's *Jupiter Courier* quit after charging that the parent Scripps Co. ordered a slant on political coverage; and the *Tacoma News Tribune* in Washington accepted a writer's resignation after editors could not locate a number of people he had quoted. The *Sacramento Bee* (California) called for the resignation of a former Pulitzer Prize–winning columnist when editors could not determine that the individuals mentioned in several of her man-on-the-street columns were real. Multimedia star and columnist Mitch Albom of the *Detroit Free Press* wrote about two Michigan State basketball players who told him they would attend an NCAA semifinal game, but changed their minds. His sports story, written in advance about their attendance, was incorrect, but his editors decided to forgive him, in part, because of the prestige he brings to the Midwestern publication.

"It is a depressing time for lovers of newspapers and the old world of print journalism," columnist Kathleen Parker wrote in Florida's *Orlando Sentinel* (6/23/04). "It is also hard not to wonder whether, in seeking explanations and solutions, we're suffering from self-delusion and denial."

Journalism classes will be debating for years the merits of reporter/editor involvement in the thirty-year-old BTK multiple-murder case in Wichita, Kansas. Journalists passed on communications from the serial killer to authorities, often honoring police requests to suppress information.

Los Angeles Times media critic Tim Rutten, commenting on the BTK case (3/5/05), asked, Were the Wichita reporters behaving ethically when they complied with authorities' requests to withhold information from their readers and viewers?

"Of course they were. In the general course of things, it's obviously true that newspapers and broadcasters should not allow government officials to dictate what they report. But murder investigations, particularly those involving sadistic, demented serial killers, hardly occur in the general course of things. An ethical system that dictates that you should never cooperate with authorities is as destructive as one that says you must always cooperate."

Rutten added, "First of all, it's important to remember that whatever they may or may not be, journalistic ethics are not like those that govern law, medicine, or architecture. The so-called learned professionals license their members and operate according to legal statutes that set standards of education and training and impose written codes of conduct binding on all license holders. Our constitutional guarantee of a free press precludes such arrangements, because the First Amendment's rights belong to individuals and not institutions. Thus, journalism is a vocation, rather than a profession. Nobody gets to set up standards of admission or practice because journalism is the public expression of a right enjoyed by everyone who lives under the rule of the U.S. Constitution."

In an aside, Rutten said that those who argue that computer "bloggers" deserve the same legal protection as newspaper reporters and network anchors are simply "out to lunch."

The Jayson Blair story, which shook the *New York Times* to its core, involved a young black reporter with an apparent substance-abuse problem who lied and deceived his editors and the newspaper's readers for months in 2003–4. The discovery of his journalistic "crime spree" ultimately led to the resignations of Executive Editor Howell Raines and Managing Editor Gerald Boyd in a major shake-up at the newspaper. It also caused extensive discussion about the affirmative action in the nation's newsrooms.

Blair wrote a book about his side of the story entitled *Burning Down My Masters' House* (New Millennium, 2004). In it, he said, "I lied and I lied . . . and then I lied some more. I lied about where I had been. I lied about where I had found information. I lied about how I wrote the story. And these were no everyday little white lies . . . they were complete fantasies, embellished down to the tiniest made-up detail. I lied about a plane flight I never took, about sleeping in a car I never rented, about a landmark on a highway I had never been on. I lied about a guy who helped me at a gas station that I found on the Internet. . . . I lied about a house I had never been to and decorations and furniture in a living room I had seen only in photographs in an archive maintained by *Times* photo editors. In the end-justifies-the-means environment I worked in, I had grown accustomed to lying."

The Blair case was followed by the misconduct at *USA Today* of Jack Kelley, a veteran foreign correspondent and one of the paper's star reporters, who had apparently been fabricating stories around the world for more than a decade.

An internal probe of the matter conducted by a team of reporters and editors determined that Kelley had invented substantial portions of at least eight important stories over ten years and "conspired to mislead those investigating his work" by asking foreign translators he employed to obfuscate the probe. Kelley resigned in January 2004. In the fallout, the paper's editor, Karen Jurgensen, and Executive Editor Brian Gallagher were replaced along with others.

USA Today's respected founder, retired Gannett Chief Executive Al Neuharth, blamed Kelley's longtime deception on the editors. "When big-time blunders occur in any workplace, the boss or bosses usually are at fault. Not reporters. The buck stops with the boss."

Nor were the media scandals confined to newspapers. CBS News compounded earlier coverage problems during the 2004 presidential campaign by carrying a controversial story on President Bush's National Guard service on *60 Minutes II*. An independent panel issued a 224-page report recommending that a producer and three others on the show be dismissed, and they were. Veteran journalist, anchor, and managing editor of the evening news Dan Rather announced his retirement before the panel issued its report, but the circumstances unquestionably left a stain on his illustrious career. CBS later announced that the midweek *60 Minutes II* would be dropped because of declining viewership. But the returns are not all in on the Dan Rather episode and the president's war record is yet to be told.

Discussing CBS's and similar situations, retired commentator Bill Moyers said, "I believe that journalism is all about writing in the sand and whistling in the wind. The wind blows the sound away and the sand flows over the writing. A journalist has impact on his time, if he's lucky."

Besides, Moyers asked, who remembers the legacy of the pioneering broadcast news greats, such as producer Fred Friendly and reporter Ed Murrow of CBS? Murrow, still an icon in American broadcast journalism, built his reputation during World War II by reporting from London rooftops on the sights and sounds of the German bombing of the city. With Friendly, he worked at CBS from 1935 to 1961.

"What's happened to the house that Murrow built?" Moyers asked. "It's now a shack by the side of the road." Moyers was referring to cutbacks at all the networks of news airtime, foreign bureaus, and correspondents. CBS ranked third in news ratings in 2005 behind ABC and NBC.

Even Russian President Vladimir Putin got into the act in February 2005 when President Bush chided Putin, on a European trip, for clamping down on freedom of the press in Russia. "We didn't criticize you when you fired those reporters at CBS," Putin said, indicating that both countries have had their media problems. Bush explained how he had no power to fire American journalists, but Putin had made his point.

During the 2004 presidential campaign, Sinclair Broadcast Group, Inc. fired Jon Leiberman, its Washington bureau chief, after he publicly protested plans for a one-sided program castigating Democratic candidate Senator John F. Kerry's anti–Vietnam War activities. Leiberman, who called the show blatant political propaganda, said he was fired for violating company policy by speaking to the media without prior corporate approval. Sinclair Broadcast Group sued Leiberman, claiming he "divulged confidential and proprietary information" to outside interests.

Another journalism scandal of a different sort erupted in late January 2005 in the form of paid-for "news" when *USA Today* reported that talk show host and conservative columnist Armstrong Williams took $240,000 from the U.S. Department of Education to promote the Bush administration's No Child Left Behind school program through his public relations firm and TV and radio appearances. Williams did not disclose his paid sponsorship to his audiences. The conservative commentator later signed a contract to be a cohost of a daily radio talk show in New York.

Asked to comment on Williams and two other writers who "moonlighted" for the government, President Bush said the White House was unaware of it, but government agencies had been told to stop the practice of secretly paying journalists because he recognized the need for independent media.

Tribune Media Services immediately dropped Williams from its stable of columnists after it was revealed that he was paid by Uncle Sam. Williams said he did not consider himself a columnist, but rather a commentator.

Later we learned the Pentagon was paying millions of dollars to a contractor to plant stories in Iraqi newspapers and bribe Iraqi opinion columnists and other journalists.

Martha Kumar, journalism professor at Towson University in Maryland, said, "It is now and always has been bad practice to blur the lines between being a journalist and serving the government in an official capacity."

The Bush administration in 2004 used similar fake video news releases to push its Medicare prescription drug plan, employing actors who pretended to be reporters. These promotional releases are produced to look like genuine news reports for TV. The Government Accountability Office (GAO) said it was a violation of the law barring use of taxpayer money to propagandize federal policies.

In a bizarre sidelight that best illustrates the confusion over who is a journalist and who isn't qualified, there is the tale of Jeff Gannon, whose real name apparently is James Dale Guckert. Gannon resigned in February 2005 as a reporter for two conservative Web sites, both owned by a Texas Republican activist. Gannon/Guckert, who attended White House press briefings and presidential press conferences on a day pass from the White House, aroused interest after he asked President Bush a question that slammed Senate Democrats and contained false information about congressional minority leader Harry Reid, a Nevada Democrat.

No longer welcomed at the White House, Gannon/Guckert said, "I've made mistakes in my past. Does my past mean I can't have a future? Does it disqualify me from being a journalist?" Maybe not, but fakery does tarnish a reporter.

In the end, it is public opinion that rewards or punishes, and journalism has received considerable criticism in the last few years as lacking in trust, responsibility, and accountability. It was once a given that of course you were an ethical person or you wouldn't have advanced as far as you had. Never mind that the pressure and increasing competition among all forms of information has made it easier to forget "get it first *but get it right.*"

Of course, deception and hypocrisy aren't new to the field. The term *yellow journalism* was coined back in the late 1800s when New York publishers Joseph Pulitzer and William Randolph Hearst sensationalized and concocted events to sell millions of newspapers.

It was Hearst who replied by telegram to illustrator Frederick Remington in Havana in 1897 when the artist got bored waiting for the outbreak of the Spanish-American War and asked to return to New York, "Please remain. You furnish the pictures and I'll furnish the war" (W. A. Swanberg, *Citizen Hearst,* Scribner, 1961).

And they both did their jobs.

Going back even further in history, Jonathan Alter, writing in *Newsweek* (2/7/05), noted that Thomas Jefferson and Alexander Hamilton each paid journalists to savage the other in print. The columnists Walter Lippmann and Ernest K. Lindley occasionally wrote speeches for Woodrow Wilson and Franklin D. Roosevelt, respectively; more recently, George Will praised Ronald Reagan's "thoroughbred performance" after a 1980 debate without disclosing that he had helped prepare Reagan for it; and Sidney Blumenthal wrote materials for Gary Hart while covering him for the *New Republic.* And paying foreign journalists and funding newspapers overseas to advance American interests has long been done by the CIA.

In the 1930s, Walter Duranty, the *New York Times* Moscow correspondent, chose to ignore the brutality of Stalin's regime, advising readers that things were calm in Ukraine when actually millions were dying of starvation.

Probably the most notorious journalism deception in the 1980s was Janet Cooke's account in the *Washington Post* of a child heroin addict, which gained her the Pulitzer Prize in 1981. Two days after receiving the award, Cooke admitted that young Jimmy, the addict, was fictitious.

During the 1990s *Wall Street Journal* reporter R. Foster Winans was convicted of securities fraud for touting stock he owned; columnist Mike Barnicle resigned from the *Boston Globe,* and another columnist, Patricia Smith, was fired from the paper for allegedly making up sources and facts; former Associated Press foreign correspondent Peter Arnett, who had a distinguished career as a combat correspondent during the Vietnam War and then Afghanistan, was fired by his later employer CNN for reading on-air a script he didn't write about an alleged event in Laos during the Vietnam War, which the government proved to be untrue.

Shattered Glass, the movie, was based on a memoir by a young reporter, Stephen Glass, who was fired from the *New Republic* after his editors discovered that he had fabricated all or parts of twenty-seven of the forty-one articles he had written for the magazine in the late 1990s. The military pulled the press credentials of TV reporter Geraldo Rivera in Afghanistan when he endangered lives by prematurely reporting upcoming troop movements.

It is not my intent here to sound like a common scold, but

after more than forty years of striving and working to succeed in journalism, I can only express my deepest sadness and regret when members of the profession don't measure up to the highest standards of integrity.

Several of the above mentioned perpetrators have apparently visited psychiatrists to learn why they cheated on stories when they didn't have to, but the basic reasons remain unclear. Money, ego, laziness, no doubt played a part as evidenced in several cases where it was easier to take shortcuts to stardom than make an effort to do the story in the right way.

Evidently, the Bob Woodward–Carl Bernstein model of hard work, checking and rechecking sources, during the Watergate scandal of the seventies seldom penetrated later journalist thinking. Their stellar examples of careful reporting and writing were brought back into the public consciousness in June 2005 when the mysterious and elusive "Deep Throat" came forth to confirm his identity as a chief source for Woodward and Bernstein in the fall of the Richard M. Nixon presidency. W. Mark Felt, ninety-one, and in failing health, was second-in-command at the FBI more than thirty years ago. He repeatedly met Woodward in the predawn hours at a public parking garage to confirm or deny allegations concerning corruption and cover-up in the Nixon administration.

There may have been controversy over Felt's aid to the reporters, but his identity as a news source was never revealed by the *Washington Post* until Felt himself talked about it. When Bob Woodward, now assistant managing editor at the *Post,* was asked how Felt's identity was kept secret for so long in gossipy Washington, he replied, "We kept that secret because we kept our word."

A few weeks before the Felt story, *Newsweek* magazine, at the government's request, rolled back a story about alleged abuse of the Koran at Guantánamo Bay in Cuba.

Richard M. Smith, chairman and editor in chief, in a letter to readers, said the magazine retracted the story "in the light of the

Pentagon's denials and our source's changing position on the allegation." He also announced tightening of editorial controls on future stories.

Ethical dilemmas and unethical journalist behavior were on the periphery of journalism in the classroom until recent years. But lately, journalism has taken a lot of hits with flagrant episodes of plagiarism, fabrication of stories, and relying on dubious documents without checking the facts.

The media will survive because as long as people are on this planet there will be news. And the proliferation of news via improved technology makes a cover-up almost impossible to maintain for long. Too many readers and too many viewers are hip to the facts and ready to catch the errors.

The record also shows that the media move rapidly to clean house because they know that their credibility is essential to their work. Heads roll when the honor of a newspaper or broadcast network is at stake.

CHAPTER 2

ERUPTIONS OF CORRUPTION

Journalists are much more preoccupied with scandals that affect presidents, public officials, and celebrities than with their own ethical misdeeds. Those stories engage the whole country and wind up in the history books. Long before the suffix *gate* was added to every political scandal, the newspapers were wallowing in the illicit and illegal behavior of public figures.

Power corrupts and scandals erupt.

There is hardly an era in American history that is not marked in some way by scandal. Even a cursory view of the many that have occurred in Washington over the years shows that the press and investigative reporters deserve the nation's accolades for the roles they played. That is why I continue to reiterate that only a free, unfettered press can save this country in its most dire moments. Too often government officials, through greed, corruption, and zest for personal power, have tried to make end runs around the law. Thanks to a courageous press, this great republic has caught up with their malevolent goals.

Whether the journalism term is *investigative reporting* or the old-fashioned description *muckraking,* it refers to the search for real or alleged corruption in government or business that can lead to publicly spotlighting the perpetrators.

Ida Tarbell was one of the original muckrakers from the late nineteenth and early twentieth centuries, who exposed and helped to shut down Standard Oil Company's virtual monopoly that stymied the ability of smaller oil companies to compete. Her father was one of the "little guys" trampled by Standard Oil's John D. Rockefeller, the company's founder, and Miss Tarbell never forgave him. Author Ron Chernow, in *Titan,* his biography of Rockefeller (Random House, 1998), said that Tarbell was a serious, well-educated journalist in an era when there weren't many women in the business. "For her, Standard Oil symbolized the triumph of grasping men over decent folk, like her father, who played fair and square," Chernow wrote.

Tarbell, writing for *McClure's Magazine,* uncovered a long-standing arrangement between Standard Oil and the railroads that led to lower freight rates for Standard Oil. Rockefeller was so incensed over her reporting he dubbed her "Miss Tarbarrel." But she got results taking on the tycoons or plutocrats of her day. Stories by her and other reporters led Congress to create the Department of Commerce and the Bureau of Corporations. The Supreme Court ruled in the case, breaking up Standard Oil and prompting a new antitrust precedent.

In a sidelight, Chernow noted that public relations for companies was still in the future, so Rockefeller took Tarbell's pounding of his reputation without ever really fighting back or giving his side of the story.

Also in Tarbell's class was Upton Sinclair, a socialist writer with a cause. He wrote a novel about immigrant workers in the Chicago slaughterhouses called *The Jungle.* After many rejections of his gloomy book, he decided to self-publish, getting an impressive number of orders, which led to publication by Doubleday. According to the National Archives it became a best seller and persuaded President Theodore Roosevelt to order an investigation of the meatpacking industry. Roosevelt met with Sinclair and told him that while he disapproved of the way the book preached socialism, he agreed that "radical efforts must be taken to do away with the efforts of arrogant and selfish greed on the part of the capitalist."

Sinclair's book inspired the passing of the Pure Food and Drug Act and the Meat Inspection Act in 1906. He went on to write many more hard-hitting books on the wrongs of society, including *The Profits of Religion* and *The Brass Check,* about newspapers. In 1943, Sinclair won the Pulitzer Prize for his novel *Dragon's Teeth,* warning about the rise of Nazism.

When I joined United Press in the summer of 1943, the name Paul Y. Anderson was still legendary for his brilliant investigative reporting for the *St. Louis Post-Dispatch.* Anderson helped to expose the Teapot Dome scandal, one of the heinous conspiracies of the early twentieth century. Anderson had already established himself as a crackerjack police reporter in St. Louis when he asked his editors to send him to Washington. When they refused, he quit and became a freelance journalist in the nation's capital, hanging out on Capitol Hill, always a better beat than the White House. After all, there are 535 legislators, many of whom want publicity for their legislation and to make a name for themselves. I do think that most of them are truly doing the public's business despite periodic eruptions of corruption.

In his great book *Reporting from Washington,* subtitled *The History of the Washington Press Corps,* Donald A. Ritchie, associate historian for the U.S. Senate, credited Anderson with "injecting muckraking into Washington journalism." While covering the Hill, Ritchie writes, Anderson "picked up rumors that something had been irregular" in the sale of naval oil reserves at Teapot Dome, Wyoming, to a private oil company. Anderson sensed the "rottenness" of Warren G. Harding's administration and began writing investigative reports about Teapot Dome for such liberal publications as the *New York Post,* the *Nation,* and the *New Republic.* Harding, an Ohio Republican, was the nation's twenty-ninth president.

Anderson also shared his findings with Montana Senator Thomas Walsh, who conducted hearings with Anderson suggesting witnesses to call and questions to ask. Walsh's inquiry uncovered evidence that Interior Secretary Albert Fall had taken a bribe from the oil industry. Banner headlines drew scores of reporters to the hearing room. Anderson's reporting on the scandal got him the job he had wanted at the *St. Louis Post-Dispatch* Washington Bureau and won him a Pulitzer Prize.

Anderson mocked the "journalistic statesmen" of his day. I can imagine how he would view Washington colleagues today who have tiptoed around the biggest deception of the American people in recent times—the falsehoods told to lead the nation into war with Iraq. Anderson gave no quarter and did what a reporter is supposed to do, go after the story at all costs. Ritchie recalled Anderson later had long drinking bouts at the National Press Club bar. But "drunk or sober," said columnist Heywood Broun, "Paul Anderson was the finest journalist of his day."

Where are the muckrakers today when Halliburton, the oil and services goliath, has a no-bid contract in Iraq and almost a monopoly on certain reconstruction projects?

President Harry S. Truman had more than his share of post–World War II scandals, mostly involving the profiteering and corruption of many of his cronies. Having risen to the Senate with the help of the notorious Pendergast machine in Kansas City, Truman, a Democrat and the nation's thirty-third president, had ridden out the storm of criticism before. But his efforts as president to shield his friends hurt him politically, driving him down in polls to his lowest approval rating.

Officials in his administration were accused of influence peddling and mishandling of government funds, leading to what was called by Republicans "the mess in Washington." His attorney general, Howard McGrath, was fired and walked out the door in tears. The scandals marred Truman's last years in office. It has been noted that only Secretary of State Dean Acheson and a few friends saw him off to his home in Independence, Missouri, on January 20, 1953, following the inauguration of President Dwight D. Eisenhower. As the years have passed, Truman's reputation has risen to historic heights because of his bold foreign policy decisions in the aftermath of World War II, and his noble move to end the outrageous discrimination against black soldiers by integrating the U.S. armed services.

During the administration of Richard M. Nixon, the *New York Times* stepped front and center when it published the Pentagon Papers, uncovering the secret dealings leading to the tragic role of the United States in the Vietnam War.

The Papers were a seven-thousand-page classified Defense Department history of U.S. involvement in Vietnam from 1945 to 1971, leaked by Daniel Ellsberg in 1971. They showed that President Johnson had intended to go to war in Vietnam even while insisting he had no such plans. The publication of selected excerpts angered President Nixon, who had succeeded Johnson, and soon-to-be Secretary of State Henry Kissinger. They went to court to enjoin publication on grounds of national security. The *Washington Post* then joined in the court case and began publishing the Papers as well.

In a 6–3 decision, the Supreme Court held that the injunctions against publication were unconstitutional prior restraints and that the government had not proved any damage to national security. It was a victory for the American people, exposing the perfidy of a war that was daily becoming more and more unpopular.

The Pentagon Papers stories won accolades for the nation's top newspapers in days when they were willing to defy the government—something we saw less and less after the start of the twenty-first century and the trauma of the 9/11 attacks on Washington, D.C., and New York. As political scandals go, Watergate, by far, was the most catastrophic episode, and it left its scars on society. It also told me a lot about the American people. It all began with a break-in at the Democratic National Committee headquarters at the Watergate office complex on June 17, 1972, just as the Nixon reelection campaign was about to go full steam ahead.

The first reports of the burglary were shrugged off until a couple of *Washington Post* metro reporters began digging and learned that one of the "burglars" carried a pocket telephone book with the numbers of some White House officials. Like a dog with a bone, they were not going to let go. They began turning up more and more evidence that the break-in was masterminded from the highest levels of government. By this time, Bob Woodward and Carl Bernstein were finding fertile ground in countless interviews with secretaries, campaign workers, and other helpful aides to government officials. But their gold mine was Mark Felt, the number two man at the FBI, whom Nixon had passed over when choosing a successor to the late J. Edgar Hoover. Woodward and Felt had struck up an earlier friendship. Felt anonymously corroborated information that the *Post* team was turning up and became famous, or infamous—depending on the point of view— as "Deep Throat." He remained anonymous until May 31, 2005, when Felt's family decided it was time to reveal the role the ninety-one-year-old former top-ranking FBI agent had played in exposing the Nixon administration's abuse of government power and helping to depose a president. The identity of Deep Throat had remained a question of deep curiosity long after Nixon had left office.

For years as I made speeches around the country about Washington political life, I was asked if I knew who he was, and my stock answer was that if I knew, I would have written it long ago. I did feel that he was an insider, but I did not indulge much in the guessing game played by former Nixon White House aides on their lecture circuits.

The handbook lesson for reporters is to find the dissident person among the ranks and establish a trustful relationship. I view Felt as a hero who did the right thing. He lines up with the many whistle-blowers who have seen government officials betraying their oaths to protect the U.S. Constitution. Sure he had personal motives, but he also obviously felt a tremendous responsibility to the country to warn against the encroaching danger of the Nixon White House.

As a White House reporter in that disgraceful era, I will always feel that I should have been more vigilant and skeptical of an administration that tried to hide its dark side. And they would have gotten away with it had it not been for the courage of Katharine Graham, publisher of the *Washington Post,* Ben Bradlee, the executive editor, and other brave souls who dared to take on the administration and to pay for an investigative team that numbered eighteen reporters. The *New York Times* also pursued the story, but the *Post* was way ahead in coverage.

After the revelations of Watergate and the political demise of Nixon, I am sure that many correspondents must have gone through the same Monday-morning quarterbacking that I did trying to retrace their missteps. I have often described those days in the pressroom as "darkness at noon," the title of one of the great books by Arthur Koestler depicting his deep disillusionment with Stalin's Communism. I was beginning to see the sinister side of the Nixon White House through the frequent, sometimes edgy, telephone calls from Martha Mitchell, while her husband, John, was attorney general in the Nixon administration and later when he headed the Committee to Reelect the President, known as CREEP.

Mrs. Mitchell first was heralded by Nixon as a fresh, outspoken popular cabinet wife who knew how to put the anti–Vietnam War protesters in their place. She became a public figure in her own right with feisty appearances on TV, unprecedented for a government official's wife. But she became Nixon's bête noire when she voiced criticism of the war and expressed fear that her husband was getting deep in the seamy side of politics, which she called "a dirty business."

On a Nixon trip from California to Washington, Martha wandered to the back of Air Force One, where the press "pool" of reporters and cameramen were ensconced, and in the chatter she said, "The Vietnam War stinks." My male colleagues picked up their pens as I did and scribbled her words on our notepads, then ran to telephones after we landed at Andrews Air Force Base. After that incident, she was barred from the presidential jet and became persona non grata with the Nixon crowd. Reporters often ridiculed her and spread the word that her spoutings in early-morning hours were alcohol-driven.

I believe she could hardly stand the deceit surrounding her and wanted to shout it out to the world. In her way she did, indeed, and is still remembered fondly by many women who have somehow identified with her over the years. She will always remain for me the prototype of the Southern woman, depicted so poignantly by playwright Tennessee Williams.

Martha found the telephone was her friend, and she learned that when she really wanted to get the word out "pronto," she could call wire-service reporters. I was fortunate enough to get her calls—at odd hours, I admit—and she even tracked me down during an appearance of mine in the West. That was the call in January 1973 when Martha told me Nixon should resign. Moments afterward, I called my UPI office in Washington and dictated an urgent story. Nixon was furious, wondering how to rein in Martha. Once one of his top henchmen ran into the street after me and said, "Why don't you get some class and hang up on Martha Mitchell?"

Although the incredible machinations of the administration were a mosaic to her and she could not put it all together (who could?), she knew that something was terribly wrong and that it would engulf her family. She loved her husband, but few marriages could have survived what they went through. John Mitchell remained loyal to Nixon even after serving a prison term. Martha died on Memorial Day in 1976. My lead: "When the parade passes by, we'll remember Martha Mitchell . . ." A funeral wreath at her gravesite read, "Martha was right."

Another major debacle that preoccupied the White House in recent times was the Iran-contra scandal, which tarnished the Reagan administration and diminished the "morning in America" atmosphere of Ronald Reagan's White House. It involved the contravention of U.S. law to send arms to Iran's Khomeini regime in exchange for money and the release of American hostages who were being held in Lebanon. More than that, most of the $30 million paid by Iran for the arms was transmitted to the contra rebels trained by the United States to overthrow the Sandinista regime in Nicaragua. Millions of dollars are still unaccounted for. National Security Affairs Director Robert McFarlane, his successor John Poindexter, and Marine Lt. Col. Oliver North ran a sub-rosa government operation from the basement offices of the Reagan White House, directing the Iran-contra activities.

When it was first exposed by the Lebanese newspaper *Ash-Shiraa,* which wrote the story of the illegal transfer of arms to Iran, Reagan was in great denial, dismissing the publication as "that rag." The irate Reagan, who first denied any knowledge of the arms deal, denounced persistent reporters as sharks circling blood in the water. The more intuitive first lady, Nancy Reagan, was in deep despair, fearing that her husband would be impeached when the scandal broke. She moved quickly, called on old political pros, Republicans and even Democrats, and cleaned house. On the advice of politically savvy Bob Strauss, a Democrat, she forced the resignation of Donald Regan, the White House chief of staff, and other aides. Reagan—for this and other reasons called "the Teflon president"—survived, and so did Vice President George H. W. Bush, who told David Broder, the correspondent-columnist for the *Washington Post,* that he was "out of the loop" during the secret meetings that had led to the arms-for-hostages scheme. Not so. The investigation of the scandal later showed Bush attended seventeen meetings of the National Security Council in preparation for the clandestine operation. You might have thought Bush, who had served in nearly every other top job in government including the directorship of the CIA, was Rebecca of Sunnybrook Farm in that era, unscathed, untouched by the seamy machinations of a second government that had been set up by Poindexter and North in the White House basement, doing what they believed was what Reagan wanted. I've always wondered why Broder did not go back to Bush and confront him about his deceptive interview, but reporters don't do that. They move on and take such dissembling in sophisticated stride. But it seems to me that the media have a responsibility to the public to retrace their steps and somehow seek the truth.

Several criminal convictions resulted from the scandal, including those of McFarlane, North, and Poindexter. McFarlane was put on two years' probation, and North and Poindexter had their convictions vacated because of immunity agreements with the Senate for their testimony. In the end, Reagan pardoned Defense Secretary Caspar Weinberger along with several CIA and State Department officials charged with withholding information on the Iran-contra fiasco.

Reagan's image was tainted for a time, but nobody in Congress wanted to impeach the aging president and he left office with his head held high. He was almost immortalized by the nation when he died in 2004 of Alzheimer's disease. Other presidents had their scandals, but not in the same class as Watergate or Iran-contra.

President Jimmy Carter had to contend with allegations against Bert Lance, his budget director, who had to divest himself of ownership interests in Georgia's Calhoun First National Bank after a 1977 Justice Department investigation of irregular practices. Lance quit the administration and faced ten counts involving alleged loans to relatives and friends as well as false financial statements. In 1980, Lance was found innocent of all charges against him.

I will always remember with affection President Carter's late brother, Billy, who was naively flattered by the attention paid to him by the Libyan government because of his status in the first family. Apparently, Carter visited Libya three times in 1978 and 1979, eventually registering as a foreign agent for the Libyan government. He received a $220,000 loan from Libyan interests, which caused an uproar, especially among Republicans hoping to unseat the president.

President Carter loved his younger brother very much and held an hour-long news conference to defend him, an excruciating and poignant ordeal. During this period, there was a sea change in what reporters were allowed to publish, especially stories dealing with the private lives of top officials.

When I started covering the John F. Kennedy administration, a golden rule had prevailed for years: the private lives of presidents and other high-ranking officials were off-limits. There were rumors galore about Kennedy's alleged flirtations and dalliances, but they did not find their way into print or broadcast under a gentleman's agreement that he had a right to privacy unless his activities affected his duties and responsibilities. For overlooking the rumors, we reporters were often accused of being protective of Kennedy. Understand, please, that it was a different era and reporters abided by the agreement. Although gossip was also rampant about previous presidents, it remained just that—gossip—and reporters did not attempt to verify it. The sexual revolution of the 1960s and the growth of tabloid journalism changed the picture.

When former Senator Gary Hart (D-Colo.) ran for the presidency in 1984, he discovered that private lives were no longer off-limits. Hart made the mistake of daring reporters to look into his personal life. They did and found him on a boat with his girlfriend, Donna Rice. The married Hart had to bow out of the race when the headlines sank his candidacy.

The only rumble President Jimmy Carter caused concerning his private life was when he admitted in a *Playboy* magazine interview that he had "lust in his heart" for certain women. Even this minimal confession made headlines at the time.

The all-absorbing scandal that occupied the nation for months was President Bill Clinton's liaison with White House intern Monica Lewinsky, which led to his impeachment by the House and an acquittal after a Senate trial. Special Prosecutor Kenneth Starr and his staff pursued the president relentlessly, and their activities made daily headlines. The Republican right peddled all sorts of innuendos about Clinton's private life. He also had to deal with charges by Paula Jones that he had made sexual overtures to her in his hotel room when he was governor of Arkansas and revelations by Gennifer Flowers of a longtime relationship with him in Little Rock. It all served to make the most personal aspects of his life fair game for the media and followed him to Washington.

Only his resilience and a strong belief in himself helped him to ride out the storm, but it was a page-turner for the country while it lasted. Clinton was not alone under the heavy cloud of scandal, and other politicians learned that they were no longer able to hide their assignations; it was no-holds-barred for the media who covered them. Officials also quickly discovered that even if the mainstream press resisted writing about their private lives, the tabloids and cable broadcasts would not exercise the same restraint. Once the story is on the public record, other media must follow suit and carry the story or be accused of covering up. If they deliberately skip the story, computer bloggers—the new electronic vigilantes—will berate them for the omission.

President Bill Clinton never knew a second in the White House when he was not being investigated. The GOP ultraconservatives denied him legitimacy from the moment he took office. It started with the investigation of Whitewater. Back in the 1970s Clinton and his wife, Hillary, purchased shares in a real estate venture backed by Madison Guaranty Savings and Loan, which went bankrupt in 1989. There were accusations against the Clintons involving improper campaign contributions, tax benefits, and political favors. The Clintons denied any wrongdoing and, in fact, claimed they had lost money in the deal.

A special prosecutor, Kenneth Starr, as relentless as the policeman Javert in the book *Les Misérables,* took over the Whitewater investigation. He won authorization to expand the probe when in an unrelated matter Clinton lied about an Oval Office liaison with twenty-one-year-old White House intern Monica Lewinsky.

Whitewater faded into the woodwork while the GOP had a

heyday with Starr presenting his case for Clinton's impeachment for his perjury in connection with the Lewinsky affair. In 1998, while investigating Clinton's sexual indiscretions, Starr indicated his office had no impeachable evidence in the Whitewater case. It ended when another prosecutor, Robert Ray, said there was insufficient evidence of a crime in the Whitewater inquiry.

The news of the Lewinsky affair broke in January 1998 on the Drudge Report Web site, although *Newsweek* magazine had the story, but had not yet printed it. Clinton issued a series of denials and, in the White House Roosevelt Room, with his wife present, declared, "I did not have sexual relations with that woman, Miss Lewinsky." He said he had never lied about it and the allegations were false.

The scandal burgeoned, of course. Sex is more intriguing than financial corruption, and Clinton's political enemies were savoring his downfall. In May 1998, a federal judge ruled that his Secret Service agents could be compelled to testify to a grand jury. On December 19, 1998, the House of Representatives passed articles of impeachment against Clinton for perjury and for obstruction of justice by votes of 228–206 and 221–212.

The House vote forced Clinton to stand trial in the Senate. On February 12, 1999, the Senate rejected both articles of impeachment. The perjury charges were rejected 55–45 and obstruction of justice was rejected 50–50. Clinton rode out the storm and left the White House on January 20, 2001, bloody but unbowed. He never lost his popularity with the American people, though he fell in the esteem of many.

But if ever there was a comeback politician, it certainly was Clinton, who abided by the same family philosophy that had kept Nixon going after the Watergate ordeal: never give up. Both Clinton and Nixon took that advice literally from their attentive mothers.

CHAPTER 3

PRESIDENTS AND REPORTERS— NEVER THE TWAIN SHALL MEET

Reporters are accused of being adversarial—particularly with politicians. You bet we are. And, we are accused of harping only on the bad news—the scandals. Not true. Tell us the good news and we will happily report it, too.

Even when it was quiet at the White House, I soon learned there was no such thing as a nonnews day. A slow day, perhaps, but something was always happening in somebody's time zone. I learned that the silence in the pressroom was simply the lull before the storm. News broke at all hours when I was working for a wire service on the day-to-day "body watch" of the president and his family. Many times I rushed out of my apartment after midnight to grab a cab for the White House after a hurried telephone call from my office in the National Press Building.

Sometimes it would be an important announcement from the podium in the White House Briefing Room, especially during the Vietnam War and later following the attacks on Grenada and Panama and during the first Gulf War.

There were other news bulletins as well, such as when an unauthorized helicopter landed on the South Lawn. On another occasion, the pilot of a small plane crashed into a wall near the Rose Garden of the Executive Mansion.

While some reporters found the White House beat boring and

confining, I thought there was never a dull moment. My colleagues and I covered everything for my employer, United Press International, on the premise that a news item or a presidential appointment would certainly be of interest to someone among the worldwide media clients. Every time I rushed into the Oval Office as part of the "thundering herd," as we were dubbed by President Kennedy, I knew it was a privilege. Over the years, I saw hundreds of Americans and foreign visitors peering through the White House fence, wondering what was going on and asking if the president was in residence. They would also spot the television broadcasters on the North Lawn facing Pennsylvania Avenue and figure there was big news breaking. It often was.

I have seen many changes in journalism since I began my career sixty years ago. The changes are in style, approach, and especially technology. In the "good old days," we reporters would run for blocks to get to a telephone to call a breaking story to our offices. We often knew the frustration of getting to a Western Union office to file a story only to find the office closed. The situation was much worse for war correspondents, of course, whose competitive stories might be delayed for days by censors or lack of transportation at the front. Nowadays we have moved from Teletypes and landline phones to cell phones, computers, and satellite transmission. The electronic era of instant communications is upon us, but unfortunately that doesn't mean the journalistic product is any better. Despite all the innovations, good journalism still takes a lot of legwork, and reporters know nothing can replace seeing an event unfold with their own eyes. Laptop computers are standard gear for reporters, who can file their stories anywhere and anytime.

The newsrooms have changed, too. They are funereal in their silence, sometimes described as insurance offices with carpeting on the floor and computer "pods" where each reporter sits in virtual isolation from his or her colleagues. I miss the clack-clack of the old Teletypes. The upscale, pristine offices that have now replaced the dingy workspaces that we used to call our newsrooms lack the pandemonium when big stories are breaking, and the sense of camaraderie that we all felt when we were working together. Call it nostalgia, but I miss the old excitement and urgency.

I am often asked, What took you into the news business? What made you want to be a reporter? How did I become so hooked for life by a profession where day to day there was no guarantee of security or money, only knowledge, and a feeling that I was contributing to the great cause of informing the American people of things they needed to know? Many reporters were inspired to go into the newspaper business by working on their school papers, as I was. It is a familiar story. I felt any position that would allow me to be nosy all my life was the job for me. I also loved the collegiality I found working on a college newspaper and later a daily paper. I had no great illusions then that it would be easy, but I also did not realize to what extent it was a man's world.

It was the World War II era of the 1940s and the government was drafting every young man who had a pulse. No family was spared. I graduated from college and headed for Washington. I landed a job on the now defunct *Washington Daily News,* owned by Scripps Howard Newspapers, as a copygirl, meaning a gofer. I thought I had arrived, but I only had a foot in the door. Still, I was working among the pros and learning a lot as I watched them type their stories on old manual typewriters, rip them out of the machine, and shout, "Copy!" The stories were transmitted to other Scripps papers by Teletype operators, who often would catch mistakes, so attuned were they to the news. Yes, reporters and editors did chain-smoke, and some kept a pint of liquor in the desk drawer. Some of the men even kept their hats on at a jaunty angle, just as in the Ben Hecht play and movie *The Front Page.* The newsroom was grubby and alive with gossip.

Scripps Howard had several correspondents covering the war, posted around the world. There was an air of great pride when a *Daily News* reporter would scoop the three other competitor newspapers at the time—the *Washington Post,* the *Evening Star,* and the *Times-Herald,* all gone now except for the *Post.*

Later, I joined the United Press as a writer for the local news broadcasts, going to work at 5:30 a.m. I paid my dues to the business. My job included editing and cutting national stories coming over the Teletypes to a few paragraphs to be transmitted to government agencies and news bureaus for out-of-town newspapers. When five bells would ring, I would jump from my seat to the Teletype machine and watch a bulletin being transmitted over the wire. By this time, I knew that I had chosen a demanding career that would pay little but would reward me with an education every day.

In 1957, United Press merged with a competing wire service, the International News Service, to become United Press International or UPI. As time went by, I covered the Justice Department and many downtown government agencies, including Health, Education, and Welfare (now Health and Human Services). Call me a romantic, but I look back and realize that those truly were the finest days of newspapering. The highest integrity was instilled in reporters, editors, and photographers. We could not conceive of anyone fabricating a story. There was so much news breaking and so many reporters willing to do the legwork. The atmosphere was definitely freewheeling, and reporters knew they would sink or swim by their abilities. They were on their own to get the facts. Sure, there was a lot of public relations being dispensed by the government then, but none of the organized "spin" and managed news we were to deal with years later.

I began covering President Kennedy after the 1960 election. I never revised my opinion that he was the most inspired leader of the last half of the twentieth century. Although he had only a thousand days in office before he was assassinated on November 22, 1963, I felt that he had more than made his mark in history, if only through his eloquent speeches. But there was more: the creation of the Peace Corps; the signing of the first nuclear test ban treaty; and his goal to land men on the moon in a decade, a dream fulfilled after he died. The White House press corps was relatively small. Television crews arrived in the pressroom only on special occasions, and when Kennedy instituted live televised news conferences. The atmosphere was chummy. Kennedy would walk through a large reception room where reporters and photographers lounged about and he would banter with us. His wit was ever ready, and he seemed to relish the give-and-take. In those days, we got close to a real live president, watching his ups and downs. Sure, there was secrecy, but not as much as was manifested in later administrations.

Sometimes I would arrive at the White House at 5:30 a.m. and not leave until after midnight. When there was a visit by a head of state, the president and his wife would often host a state dinner. White House reporters would cover the toasts after dinner, the entertainment in the East Room, and perhaps the "mix and mingle" after dinner where we could "buttonhole" the president and the foreign leader to ask the question of the day. Several presidents tolerated reporters covering the social events. Of course, we women were properly attired in our long gowns and elbow-length white gloves, often purchased at the local discount stores.

I had a trademark outfit, but it fit all occasions—a long, black velvet skirt, with a matching jacket, and a fancy satin or silk blouse. It became my standard uniform as I watched official wives parade in their Dior and Chanel gowns.

Some of the officials and their wives were wary of having reporters around, but we made a case for being there. We argued that the American people could enjoy the glamour of a state dinner vicariously on television and through our stories. After all, they were taxpayer-supported events. Reporters were able to learn many news notes at the White House social affairs. The big prize was to get a comment from the president on the story of the day, and amazingly, many of them did talk, perhaps because no outsiders had asked for their views all day.

I recall running to find a telephone many times when covering a social event, after learning some bit of "hard news" that I felt could not wait until the party was over. The last president I covered, George W. Bush, had no use for such social formalities. He and the first lady held only six state dinners in five years, far below the number held by his predecessors. He shunned the parties because he liked to go to bed early and also because he was a teetotaler.

The guest lists for state dinners were always fascinating. Most presidents tried to provide a mix of guests, always top officials in the cabinet, but in addition they would include Hollywood stars, politicians, prominent journalists, and many political contributors. Often, the guests would enjoy dancing in the Grand Foyer to the music of the Marine Corps Band, long after the president and his wife had taken the elevator to the family quarters. President Lyndon B. Johnson was the exception. He felt it was important for the women guests "to dance with the president" so they could go home and tell their friends. Besides, he liked to dance.

On the rarest occasions I have been invited to the family quarters. Johnson used to spot a reporter and ask if we had had lunch. We always said no, of course. He would escort us to the upstairs family dining room to join him in a light repast. He was kept on a strict diet because he'd suffered a heart attack in the midfifties. Not that LBJ stuck to his diet, but his wife, Lady Bird, closely watched what he consumed.

Johnson liked people around him at all times. At a private lunch, he would read aloud the transcripts from the news briefing held earlier in the morning. He would name the reporter who asked the toughest question. He had us all pegged. Johnson was very aware of what was being written about him. Many presidents were, including Kennedy, but others seemed detached and immune to news reports unless they were very critical.

I was invited to a state dinner as a guest by nearly every president I covered. On those evenings I would don my best party clothes, show up, and wave at my colleagues who were behind the ropes as I had so often been. It was my night and I made the most of it. I carried a small notebook, but it was hidden. After all, I was a guest, but that did not stop me from trying to get some news, surreptitiously of course. There was never a time when I didn't feel that I was sharing a moment in history on those special occasions, but when you are a guest at the White House, you adhere to the protocol of the evening.

I remember covering a St. Patrick's Day dinner at the White House. The first lady, Jacqueline Kennedy, was out of town. The president's mother, Rose Kennedy, looking every bit the queen as she presided as hostess, was resplendent in a green and gold brocade gown. Kennedy observed the group of newswomen checking up on the guests, and I remarked to him, "It's a great night for the Irish." He grinned and quipped, "What are you doing here?" My ancestry is Syrian/Lebanese. It was wonderful to observe presidents lighten up on social evenings at the White House. For some, it seemed to be fun. For others, it was an ordeal to entertain, but they knew it was part of the job so they would grin and bear it. Their toasts, usually written by their own speechwriters or someone from the State Department, were always effusive in praising the visiting head of state and his country.

No president ever failed to thank a French VIP visitor for the contributions of the Marquis de Lafayette, who fought in the American Revolution. During the Cold War, when the policy of coexistence with the Soviet Union seemed like a happy possibility, we watched for any sign of a thaw in relations. We avoided diplomatic nuances, but we could tell if two leaders were talking amiably or wearing frowns. Most of the time, they would go out of their way to show that they had common ground and were opening a new era of friendship.

I flew on Air Force One, the presidential plane, more than any other correspondent in the years I was with UPI. I made most of the major trips abroad with Nixon, Ford, Carter, Reagan, Bush-1, and Clinton, and too many trips to count with Kennedy, Johnson, and the others when they went campaigning or home for vacations. I got to know the Air Force One stewards and the crews, very kind and accommodating people. Many other reporters liked to ride the more relaxing, more fun, chartered press plane. I preferred the presidential jet to the press plane, not for the honor of being a passenger, but because I was working. If there was a story on the trip, it was on Air Force One.

Those foreign trips were memorable. Every reporter wanted to be on them. They were exhausting and exhilarating. Sometimes we would spend only twenty-four hours in a country or two days at most. Often it seemed we were reduced to arrivals and departures. Seeing the world leaders close up, we were able to take their measure and see whether there was any rapport between them. In her heyday, British Prime Minister Margaret Thatcher always managed to stand next to Ronald Reagan, her favorite American president, during the traditional "class picture" with the economic-summit leaders. Although I covered many of the economic-summit meetings, it seemed that yet another Middle East crisis would interrupt deliberations on third world debt or other global fiscal problems.

In the past, when the Arab countries were friendlier, thousands would turn out along the route with smiles and welcoming signs to see an American president. If there were strong security problems, a presidential motorcade would zip nonstop through the main streets of the capital and get a wave from a bystander or two. I learned early on that in most countries, welcoming ceremonies for an American president were staged. If the president was personally popular, the crowds turned out without prompting.

As I make speeches around the country, I am often asked, "What was your most memorable trip with a president?" I have to admit it was the breakthrough journey to China in 1972 with President Nixon. The United States and China had no relations and no formal contacts for twenty years. It was like landing on Mars. Everything was a story and every correspondent in Washington wanted to be on that trip. The world was stunned when

Nixon went on television to announce he had been invited to China. Taiwan, where the Chinese Nationalist government was installed, was not happy. Japan was shocked at not being informed beforehand.

For us, it was strong evidence that reporters do often write the first draft of history. Americans and the rest of the world got a look at the new Communist-controlled China through our eyes. We were treated royally, but watched carefully. We, in the media, attended banquets with the president and the official party. We had incredible access for the stories we were to write.

As the years went on, more and more barriers were erected because of security threats and fears, impeding open coverage of a president. We used to tag along when a president walked through a hotel lobby or took a stroll. No more. All that changed as time went on, and more so after the 9/11 terrorist attacks on the World Trade Center in New York and on the Pentagon. There was no longer any running alongside the president and tossing questions at him. In recent years, the president has been surrounded by a protective cordon of Secret Service agents at all times. A SWAT team with guns poked outside car windows rides in the motorcade. The president still gets into crowds and shakes hands, but the crowds are highly scrutinized and any potential protesters are kept away.

Whenever I get together with former White House reporters to discuss old times, we realize that we had the advantage of close proximity to the president that may never happen again. It seems unlikely that the White House will return to the days when President Harry S. Truman took his morning strolls down Pennsylvania Avenue at dawn with a couple of reporters and photographers in tow. That would be a dangerous exercise for any president once his routine was known. Somehow, still, we feel it is absolutely necessary that reporters be on hand when a president is in public, just in case. It is important to have an objective observer present to counteract aides who might want to twist or gloss the facts.

A few years ago, Jon Frandsen, a newspaperman and my friend of many years, gave me a copy of a book his father, Julius Frandsen, the late Washington bureau chief of UPI, cherished. It was published in 1948 and is simply a letter by John H. Sorrels. Sorrels was executive editor of Scripps Howard newspapers and wrote to a young student at Stanford University who was considering entering the newspaper business. Sorrels wrote, in part, "It seems to me that the newspaper business would prove inadequate and unsatisfactory to anyone who considers it merely the means of earning a living, because the newspaper is more than a business, or a trade, or a profession. It's a way of life." I am hoping that the new generation of journalists who come along will understand the role of journalism in a democracy and put it back on the pedestal where it belongs.

CHAPTER 4

PRESS SECRETARIES—IN THE BULL'S-EYE

For many reporters, the White House beat was nirvana—the top of the mark.

More than any president, we came to know and size up the press secretaries. My favorites had wit, warmth, and compassion, understanding that each—press secretary and reporter—had a role to play. The country was best served when the press secretary also understood he or she was dealing with the nation's business, operating as a publicist for the president.

I have always thought that the job of White House press secretary is the toughest position after the presidency itself.

In fact, an *impossible job* might be a better description because the press secretary is caught between two worlds—an administration that wants to paint a rosy picture, no matter what the facts, and a skeptical, perhaps cynical press corps that is seeking truthful answers. Faced often with this dilemma and with job survival at stake, most press secretaries have opted for the political rule: to get along is to go along with whatever the president or his top aides want publicly said—whether it's right or wrong.

Unfortunately, too few who have served in that exalted office have risen to the occasion and been willing to defy the Oval Office in the interests of honesty. Integrity, credibility, perhaps a good conscience, and definitely a sense of humor are the qualities that make a great press secretary, in my opinion. That is why there have been so few.

The press secretaries I have observed over the years take the White House podium with the best of intentions, assuming they do not have a built-in hostility to the media after the long, hard road to the White House. I have even heard them say, "I will never lie to you." I smile when I hear that. I do believe, however, that some kept that promise, knowing how fast a lie can catch up to them, even defying presidents who wanted to shade the truth.

By the time a press secretary gets to the White House, the press corps is usually divided into friend or foe. There usually are a fair number of media sycophants versus what presidential aides have over decades termed "the enemy."

It is true, as President John F. Kennedy used to say, that when a press secretary steps into the pressroom, he is in the bull's-eye.

Historically, Franklin Delano Roosevelt's first press secretary, Steve Early, gave structure to the role and established it as a formal position with the White House, although earlier presidents had spokesmen who handled the public side of their administrations. To this day, Early wears the crown for keeping the press abreast of developments and keeping a strong-minded president trusting and satisfied.

Some press secretaries have had experience in the news business and have a natural savvy to know when a question is coming from left field. Some try to wing it, to their sorrow.

Marlin Fitzwater, who served longest as White House spokesman—from 1983 to 1993 on the Reagan and Bush-1 staffs—said, "No one else knows the terror of facing reporters every day on every subject in the world. A spokesman can bumble the facts, freelance a question, and land in a lot of trouble."

Many of the press secretaries I have known during the nine presidencies I have covered wrote about me and quoted me in their memoirs, some favorably, some not. This chapter is simply my appraisal of how each did his job and how they could perhaps have done it better given the circumstances at the time.

The first White House press secretary I covered daily was Pierre Salinger, a bon vivant former newspaper and magazine writer, who certainly fit into the dynamic, fresh new spirit that John F. Kennedy and his clan brought to the White House: the New Frontier.

The bushy-browed Salinger loved to chomp on a cigar in his moments of relaxation, and a glint of merriment and mischief was often in his eyes when he spoke with reporters. In a way, he seemed to be saying, "We're all in it together." At thirty-five, Salinger was the youngest person ever to hold the White House press secretary position.

I covered Kennedy's inauguration and nearly every day of his brief time in office along with my colleagues the late Pulitzer Prize–winning journalist Merriman Smith and Al Spivak, now retired. There was never a dull moment.

I had the honor of closing one of Kennedy's news conferences with a "Thank you, Mr. President." And I recall his memorable "saved by the bell" look when he responded with relief, "Thank *you*, Helen."

Media relations under Salinger took a more lively turn compared to the "steady as you go" years with President Dwight D. Eisenhower and his band of successful multimillionaire business advisers. After all, Salinger was working for a president who would hit the ceiling if he saw a story about his three-year-old daughter, Caroline. At the same time, he wanted several copies of the picture that went with the written feature. Even more irate was Jacqueline Kennedy, who resented the intrusion on family privacy. It soon fell to "Lucky Pierre," as he was known, to handle media relations in both the East and West Wing, resolving tensions between Jackie's desire to maintain family privacy and a press corps that knew that every time the First Lady moved, she made news. As a public figure, she had the people mesmerized by her mystique.

Just weeks before Kennedy was sworn in, Salinger announced a major innovation: presidential news conferences on live television.

"This would give the whole nation a chance to see the president as he actually answers the questions of reporters," Salinger said at the time. "We think it would be beneficial to the press." Then, understanding Kennedy's appeal as demonstrated in the legendary Kennedy-Nixon debates, Salinger added, "And, indeed, we think it would be beneficial to all concerned."

Salinger also turned the White House into an open beat: reporters could interview any member of the White House staff on any subject without first having to clear it with the press secretary. In addition, he eliminated the rule that if one reporter got a story, all reporters got it. No more pack journalism.

In a 1974 interview with the *Los Angeles Times,* Salinger said, "There had been a practice back to the days of Steve Early [FDR] that got everyone the same information. That tended to turn reporters into robots sitting around waiting for the press secretary to tell them something. It was healthier if they could get the news on their own."

In his memoirs, Salinger said he faced the problem of the administration withholding information from him during planning for the abortive Bay of Pigs incident, the failed 1961 invasion of Cuba designed to overthrow Fidel Castro.

"I was completely shut out of the Bay of Pigs," Salinger said later. "I didn't learn about the invasion until three hours before it happened. It made dealing with the press very difficult. During a crisis, a press secretary has to be involved in the inner discussions, so he knows what can be said and what can't be said."

When the Bay of Pigs incident was over, Salinger went to President Kennedy and told him that his (the press secretary's) effectiveness would be destroyed unless he knew about even the most covert government operations. Kennedy agreed and it never happened again.

Indeed, during the Cuban missile crisis in 1962, Salinger was present at all key planning meetings, which allowed him to effectively deal with the media. He played a far greater role than press secretaries in most administrations.

After Kennedy's assassination in 1963, Salinger served his successor, Lyndon Baines Johnson, for a time, then turned to broadcast journalism. He died at his home in France in 2004 at the age of seventy-nine.

I would be remiss if I didn't pay tribute to the late Joe Laitin, who came to Washington in 1963 to serve in the Kennedy administration and stayed on as an assistant press secretary in the White House under Johnson.

Laitin, a former UPI and Reuters newspaperman, was a high government spokesman during six presidencies. In his obituary, the *Washington Post* noted that "in an extraordinary career, Laitin was an adviser to some of the most powerful people of the day, a witness to events great and small, a valued news source who seemed to know everybody from Hollywood to the White House and a legendary survivor in the bureaucratic jungles of Washington." He was a valued friend of mine who won my admiration by successfully being able to transform his consider-able abilities as a newsman to become one of the most trusted people in government. He had a marvelous mixture of wit and wisdom.

I laugh now when I review the complacency of the press at the litany of lies the Bush-2 administration told to take the United States into war with Iraq compared to the consternation of the Washington press corps when Kennedy's assistant secretary of defense, Arthur Sylvester, former correspondent for the now defunct *Newark Evening News,* said in a speech before the New York chapter of the journalism fraternity Sigma Delta Chi, in New York on December 7, 1962, "I think the inherent right of the government to lie to save itself when faced with nuclear disaster is basic."

I can well remember the brouhaha Sylvester created when he reasserted the government's right to lie. The issue is moot now.

Reporters are no longer appalled at the canards they hear at the White House.

The cliché around Washington for years was that a diplomat is a man who is sent abroad to lie for his country. This remark may be harsh, but unfortunately, reporters all too often take false statements in stride and repeat them like stenographers. I ask myself almost daily why the media in Washington has become so compliant, complicit, and gullible. It all comes down to the 9/11 terrorist attacks in Washington and New York that led to fear among reporters of being considered "un-American" or "unpatriotic."

Johnson was master of his own press relations, and if he shaded the truth at times, well, so be it. That was a president's prerogative—maybe, but reporters would not let up on Johnson when he tried to fuzzy up federal-deficit figures and sell the no-win Vietnam War.

A micromanager, Johnson could barely stand for anyone to speak for him. As a consequence, he had a series of press secretaries. After Salinger left, Johnson selected George Reedy as his press secretary. For Reedy, it was a baptism of fire. He was serving LBJ—a man bigger than life.

Reedy understood a reporter's needs and did the best he could to convey Johnson's supersecret travel plans to them. When it was suspected that Johnson would be headed for his Texas ranch on a weekend, Reedy would tell reporters, "A prudent man would pack." I kept a bag packed all the time to keep up with the impromptu president.

To cover Johnson as a reporter was to take part in a three-ring circus. He wanted the media on his side in all things, but he also was wary of what he considered our capability to harm his image. His paranoia was at its height when he tried to hide the simplest information on his comings and goings as president. Yet, it was not unusual for him to invite a reporter to ride with him in his limousine when he wanted company. I did . . . and dined out on the fact. He frequently invited members of the media upstairs to the White House family quarters to join him for lunch. I know of no other presidents, including Roosevelt, who were that hospitable in the off-limits of the family quarters.

Reedy was well aware that Johnson had a love-hate relationship with the press. He told Reedy that he wanted a story on the front page every day—a positive one, of course. Johnson, with a bank of telephones at his fingertips, personally called the late-night desk at UPI once to note that a conference he was supporting was listed on the schedule as available for a "fee" instead of for "free." Johnson was polite, but he asked for a correction, which the startled newsman granted immediately to the president of the United States.

Often, Reedy would be giving a news briefing in his office when the phone would ring from none other than POTUS (president of the U.S.). Johnson would be on the line correcting what Reedy had just told reporters. Reedy, pipe in hand, would turn ashen. Johnson was tuned in all right, and we all suspected that there was an aspect of "Big Brother" in the press briefing room.

Later, Reedy wrote a classic novel about a president with monarchial ambitions called *The Twilight of the Presidency.* Johnson never spoke to him again.

Reedy was succeeded by Bill Moyers, who had been a reporter in his teens in his hometown of Marshall, Texas, and later became a Baptist minister. Moyers was articulate and understood Johnson with all his insecurities, but as time went on, he turned against the Vietnam War, much to Johnson's disgust. Whenever Moyers entered the Cabinet Room, Johnson would say, "Here comes Mr. Stop-the-Bombing."

After the White House, Moyers became publisher of the Long Island, New York, newspaper *Newsday,* and started on a long, immensely successful career as one of the great journalists of our time. He later went to the Public Broadcasting Service, where he broadcast an in-depth program called *NOW.* Now retired, Moyers won thirty Emmy Awards for his programs.

Johnson's last press secretary at the White House was George

Christian, a fellow Texan and a pro who knew his way around politics. He had previously served as a spokesman for Texas Governor John Connally. Christian had a calming effect on Johnson and the press corps. The reporters trusted him, and although he had to suffer the presidential wrath when Johnson became enraged at reading a critical story, Christian seemed to find the best balance between serving Johnson and serving the public.

He understood Johnson's frustrations, especially when the anti–Vietnam War public protests and picketing grew so loud and so strong that Johnson couldn't venture outside the White House compound except to visit military bases and aircraft carriers.

Christian died in 2002, long after LBJ's own death. In a statement, Lady Bird Johnson and her daughters said, "The Johnson family has had many a crisis all made better because of George's wisdom, judgment, humor, and patience."

In many ways, Nixon's handpicked press secretary, Ronald Ziegler, turned out to be a tragic figure. Ziegler was a protégé of fellow Californian H. R. Haldeman. Nixon's longtime friend and former press secretary Herbert G. Klein was in charge of communications for the incoming administration, but he soon learned that he did not have the clout with the president that Nixon's top aides, Haldeman and John Ehrlichman, enjoyed. This was unfortunate because Klein was a sensible man who understood Washington, Congress, and politics.

Ziegler was well aware of the touted hostility between Nixon and the press corps, dating back for years and from past elections, and he tried to bridge the gap. He also seemed to try to make the Nixon Oval Office more reporter-friendly.

It lasted awhile, but the onset of the Watergate scandals ended attempts at reconciliation. Nixon liked some reporters, but not many. He was personally just as secretive as Johnson, but he was not a "people person." Nixon could charm crowds of thousands, but he was not at home in intimate conversations with the media. Reporters were called "the enemy," and I am sure that is the way he viewed them. He even had an "enemies list" of correspondents; to appear on it became a badge of success for many journalists as the Nixon administration deteriorated.

To be fair, Nixon was brilliant in many ways. Articulate and widely traveled, he was impressive at a news conference, taking questions at a stand-up microphone instead of a podium. He needed no notes. He also had an uncanny ability to pick the winners in political contests across the land. Politics was his life.

Nixon achieved a foreign policy coup when he made his breakthrough trip to China in 1972. Every reporter in Washington wanted to be on that journey ending a twenty-year hiatus in which the United States and China had no formal relations. I was lucky to be on that trip, an eye-opener in which the traveling reporters, photographers, and broadcasters felt they had suddenly become foreign policy experts.

Nixon held regular news conferences until the Watergate scandal began to unravel in 1973–74, when the questions became too excruciating.

Nixon was able to carry on his 1972 personal reelection campaign, but after the investigation, there was hell to pay as the Watergate scandal unfolded. It fell to Ziegler to answer the demanding questions every day; he originally dismissed the break-in of the Democratic National Committee headquarters at the Watergate complex as "a third-rate burglary." It was a painful time for Ziegler—so much so that he went into hiding, closing his office door to reporters and leaving his deputy, Gerald Warren, to field the tough questions. The White House drama became more and more of what seemed like a Greek tragedy.

A couple days before Nixon aides Haldeman and Ehrlichman resigned, a reporter asked Ziegler, "Is everything you have said for the last nine months inoperative?" Ziegler nodded yes.

White House press secretaries would quit, suffering from

burnout and maybe the beating they had taken from the press. Some, like Marlin Fitzwater, stayed the course and somehow were able to remain untainted.

But the real champ to me was Jerry terHorst, a Washington correspondent with the *Detroit News* who had been covering Washington for twenty-nine years. TerHorst lasted as President Gerald R. Ford's press secretary for one month, then he found he had been lied to and felt his credibility was sullied among his longtime colleagues in the media.

Later, Ford's top aides said that terHorst was not kept informed because they knew he was honest and had too many friends in the press corps. He quit on principle even though he had a family to support and an uncertain future. Even in the short time he served, terHorst was a model press secretary. He knew what reporters wanted to know and he was not afraid to tell them. They don't make them like that anymore. That is why he will always stand out in the galaxy of good press secretaries in my book. In 1974, he told reporters that Ford would seek the presidency in 1976. Others would have parried and waited for Ford to announce that he would run.

TerHorst was followed by Ron Nessen, a former UPI reporter and NBC-TV correspondent. The first day on the job, Nessen stepped up to the podium and declared, "I will never lie to you."

I am not sure whether he was able to keep that promise, but I do know that his tenure was troubled. He did not serve Ford well by his constant badgering of reporters who wrote about Ford's mishaps. He made it too personal in relations with reporters he found to be too persistent.

Nessen meant well, but he found it difficult to accommodate Ford's top aides, including Secretary of State Henry Kissinger, who was still trying to reinvent White House history. Nessen had to overcome Kissinger's braggadocio that he made 95 percent of the foreign policy in the Ford White House.

Jody Powell, with his Southern drawl and irreverence, made many friends on the campaign trail during Jimmy Carter's cam-

paign, and he was elevated to the high-profile post of press secretary when Carter moved into the White House.

Powell, who was sharp, witty, and facile with a phrase, survived in the job during Carter's four years, even though some of
Carter's advisers were urging that he be replaced. Powell was as
close to a president as an aide could get. When Carter bled, Powell bled.

However, Powell was not above wisecracking that his boss
was "tight as a tick" with money. Still, Powell was part of the
"Georgia Mafia," the outsiders who ran against Washington and
were never really accepted there.

For his part, Carter gave the press a wide berth. He was not
your hail-fellow-well-met type, bantering with reporters, but
one felt his deep sincerity and courage. A literate and erudite
man from Plains, Georgia, Carter performed at news conferences with all the facts and figures at his fingertips. He spoke in
complete sentences that had a beginning, a middle, and an end.
Carter did not suffer fools gladly. He had a sense of humor, but
he hid it, and he was not as outgoing as some of the more lovable
members of his family who embarrassed him periodically.

When Powell's White House days were over, he became a
Washington political "insider" and a wealthy man who ran a
successful public relations firm. He did not go home to Vienna,
Georgia. Presidents do go home; there is no place for them in
Washington. But the neophytes they bring with them, who
stopped to smell the roses, rarely leave.

When President Reagan entered the White House, he brought
with him a team, most of whom had made the long march with
him from California during the campaign and were kept shielded
from intimate contact with the press.

His news conferences on prime time were well staged, and
even when he hesitated on the answers, he did not lose the presidential aura and command. He boned up for those news conferences, taking briefing books the size of telephone books to Camp
David, the presidential retreat in the Catoctin Mountains of

Maryland, on the weekends before he met with the media. There's no question he was "scripted," yet his years in broadcasting as a sports reporter and in Hollywood before the camera stood him in good stead when he was onstage.

I never learned who played me or the irrepressible Sam Donaldson, one of the best in the business, when Reagan went to the ground-floor White House theater to rehearse. He would be peppered by staff with predictable questions. I was flattered at times when I was told that President Reagan asked what I was thinking or asking about events of the day.

Reagan chose James Brady, an experienced Washington hand who knew his way around the political shoals, as his press secretary. He caused consternation in the Reagan camp and hilarity among environmentalists once when he joked about "killer trees" after Reagan said that trees caused pollution.

Still, Brady gave me a heads-up occasionally, including a tip on an impending tax-cut proposal after I put a question to him privately. I was grateful for his trust.

His briefings were fun, only to be short-lived when he caught a bullet in his head intended for Reagan in an assassination attempt by John Hinckley Jr. in March 1981, less than three months after he had settled into the role of White House press secretary. Brady made a remarkable recovery, but he was incapacitated by his immobility, although his mind returned razor sharp.

Reagan graciously allowed Brady to keep his title during his eight years in the presidency, and the mantle of day-to-day briefing of the press fell to Larry Speakes. He coveted the press secretary title, but it was never bestowed on him.

Speakes did do the job, but he also did all he could to undermine David Gergen, who headed White House communications and at times took the podium himself to brief reporters. A gut fighter from Mississippi who had been trained on Capitol Hill, Speakes would deride Gergen behind his back and call him "tall," which conveyed more meaning to reporters than Gergen's height.

Gergen eventually departed the scene and Speakes was left to fend off questions about the impending Iran-contra scandal (selling arms to Iran and using the money to support Nicaraguan rebels), as well as Reagan's bout with colon cancer.

Speakes had to deal with those closest to the president, including image-maker Michael Deaver and First Lady Nancy Reagan, who feared the word *cancer* would hurt her husband's presidency.

Because of this, Speakes found it tough to cope with the press corps. At one point, he was so harassed that he dropped a stack of White House press releases in the pressroom and ran back to his office without comment.

There was no moaning at the bar when he decided to leave.

Marlin Fitzwater, who had been handling press relations for Vice President George Herbert Walker Bush, stepped into the breach.

He stayed in the job for Reagan and through the succeeding Bush presidency, ten long years. Fitzwater was well respected, but he had that sine qua non that every press secretary should have—access to the Oval Office at critical times. The president clued him in, and he could brush past other top aides who might have an ax to grind against the media.

As he makes clear in his book *Call the Briefing! A Memoir,* he was not overjoyed to see me sitting outside his office when he arrived at work each morning.

On the other hand, I gave him clues on the story he would have to contend with at his regular 11 a.m. briefing. Fitzwater was not a spinner. He also stayed within the parameters without seeming to be an automaton taking orders from topside at every turn.

As he said in his book, "Even as White House colleagues tried to goad me into privately criticizing the press for their political beliefs, I had trouble doing it, feeling instead that reporters are complex personalities who generally have reasons for writing."

He went on to describe the scene inside the White House

where "every reporter was denigrated as belonging to liberal or conservative factions."

Somehow we knew that Fitzwater was a straight shooter, but those trying to guide his public pronouncements often were not. During the first Persian Gulf War, Fitzwater was often kept informed and stayed on top of developments. He had his moments with some of the staff who preferred to keep reporters in the dark—but often he prevailed.

He wrote, "The one quality that sets journalists apart from almost everyone is their intense belief in the value of journalism."

The first President Bush had been involved in government so long that he knew most of the White House reporters by name and generally was friendly and informal. He actually much preferred the cameramen, whom he called "photodogs" with affection.

He liked informal news conferences where he could pop into the White House pressroom and take questions off-the-cuff for perhaps an hour, handling himself well. He did not enjoy prime-time news conferences and held few of them.

When his presidency ended, his more acerbic wife, Barbara, was vocal in her feelings and blamed the media for her husband's loss to Bill Clinton in 1992.

At times, Bush could be demeaning, calling the late Sarah McClendon, one of the best-known correspondents in Washington, a "squeaky wheel" when she shouted to get her questions to him acknowledged.

In a revealing moment, Fitzwater said in his book that from the moment a reporter enters the White House gate, the press is "totally controlled." He also described the media as "an unwanted appendage, like a cocklebur that attaches to your pants leg."

Fitzwater spoke of trying to deflect questions on the burgeoning problem of the Iran-contra scandal, especially after Reagan and Secretary of State George P. Shultz had emphatically pounded on the podium, saying that they would never deal with Iran.

Fitzwater also recalled another incident before a press briefing when he asked Roman Popadiuk, the White House deputy in charge of foreign affairs, "What have you got on the foreign side?"

To which Popadiuk responded, "[Senator] Sam Nunn says we're trying to reinterpret the ABM [anti-ballistic missile] Treaty so we can test Star Wars."

"Are we?" Fitzwater asked.

"Probably," Popadiuk replied, "but we're saying no."

When Fitzwater protested that he did not know anything about foreign policy and that with one word he would be making policy, he asked what he should say.

Popadiuk replied, "I'll write it up. You stick to it. Read it. No matter what they ask, just reread it."

I can't remember how many times I saw that advice in action on other matters at other times. Just read the falsehood and, when asked again, just repeat it.

But with all due respect, I think Fitzwater did a creditable job serving the nation, the presidents, and the press under constant pressure and many crises.

Some press secretaries go out of their way not to know the real story in order to protect their veracity. For them, ignorance is truly bliss. It gives them a shield and saves the presidential skin, not to mention their own.

Such was the case of Michael McCurry, press secretary to President Bill Clinton, at the height of the scandal of Clinton's liaison with White House intern Monica Lewinsky.

McCurry adopted the position "don't ask, don't tell." He did not want to know the unsavory facts, and no one behind the scenes wanted to tell him. As a result, he escaped unscathed as a Republican-instigated impeachment process against Clinton got under way.

McCurry had won high marks as a State Department spokesman who knew his way around diplomatic double-talk.

He was welcomed by White House reporters, who praised his ability to articulate the administration's positions, fence with reporters, and stay out of trouble. In the end, however, he couldn't cope with all of Clinton's personal problems.

Clinton generally was friendly to the media, but he had no close friends among them. When the Lewinsky story spread, the cable networks planted their cameras permanently on the north lawn of the White House, dubbed Monica Beach.

Clinton had to withstand personal questions from reporters including "Are you going to resign?" Brilliant in many ways, Clinton lacked "street smarts" in my opinion, although he loved being president.

When George Stephanopoulos was communications director in Clinton's first term, he tried to close off the press secretary's office to the press, a strange manifestation of arrogance for a newcomer one week on the job at the White House. He decided that reporters could no longer wander up from the so-called lower press office to his office. He closed the door and won the immediate animosity of reporters, such as yours truly, who could not believe or accept the edict.

Stephanopoulos, obviously seeking a high profile for himself, at the same time began giving the news briefings on TV. I gave him a hard time, insisting that there was no need for a press secretary since he was shutting off access. My complaints, joined by others, were heard coast to coast. Soon the door to the press secretary's office was open again.

Stephanopoulos soon had to defer the press secretary podium to Dee Dee Myers, who was glib and a member of the inner circle, but was kept out of the loop too often. She did her best, but was badly treated by Clinton's staff and didn't know Washington, which she later learned and knows now. She noted that she had lower rank, a smaller office, and less pay than any previous male press secretary.

It is an irony—but typical of Washington's proverbial revolving door—that Stephanopoulos wrote his painful memoirs, then wound up as a television talk show host and Johnny-come-lately journalist on ABC-TV.

Dee Dee Myers also came into political demand as a political pundit and contributor to *Vanity Fair.* The list of crossovers is too long to recite. Some have gone to the lesser confines, teaching journalism—of all things—at Ivy League schools.

McCurry succeeded Dee Dee and was followed by Joe Lockhart, a straight shooter. He always gave me a direct answer, no bunkum. That was Lockhart: irreverent, but unfailingly honest. Lockhart once made the point that "the ability to get in and see the president at a moment's notice is an important part of doing the job because there is a certain quality to the information you can get from the president that you can't get from someone else." He served Clinton well in the last period of his presidency.

My criticism of the press secretaries in the Bush-2 administration is that they are robots parroting the party line, on message word for word. They are afraid to deviate even when they are spouting nonsense. They stay on one page, no matter what the question.

Pleasing their president too often means more to them than their questionable responsibility to the American people; to democracy itself. They define it as loyalty to the boss, but they owe a higher loyalty to the country, in my opinion. Dissembling and avoiding the truth does not engender trust or respect. It harms the nation.

I endeared myself to President Bush-2 and his press secretary when Bush dropped into the pressroom a couple of weeks after taking office in his first term. He dutifully went down the line of reporters in the front row, where I had retained my seat on the basis of seniority. They were the regulars for the national television networks and the wire services, Associated Press and Reuters. Each of those reporters asked about Bush's top-priority tax cuts.

When the new president got to me I asked, "Mr. President,

why don't you respect the wall of separation of church and state?"

It was as if I had physically struck him.

He drew back and said, "I do," to which I responded, "If you did, you would not have a religious office in the White House. You are secular?"

"I am secular," he insisted.

A few hours later, I received a telephone call from Press Secretary Ari Fleischer, who said, "What's the idea of blindsiding the president?" I responded that I had asked a legitimate question.

I was soon to become persona non grata in the eyes of the Bush administration as I committed many more "heresies" with my questions, columns, and opinions.

Many who have served in the role of press secretary are true believers, of course—believers, that is, in the president and his course of action. But in the Bush-2 regime, it was a job requirement. Even though it was a prerequisite for the job, many should have been more troubled.

Such a man was Ari Fleischer, first press secretary to President Bush-2. His clone, Scott McClellan, was even more programmed, his answers even more automated. Fleischer started his job by saying he was an "advocate," but that in itself raised the question whether he could be fair and let the facts prevail. The question was answered in hundreds of his morning "gaggles" and afternoon televised briefings. Truth took a holiday.

The Bush-2 spokesmen were predictable and Orwellian. They lived in fear that there would be a news leak, which made Bush apoplectic, not the first president with such a reaction. Fleischer and McClellan marched in lockstep in the most secretive administration in modern history.

But even Fleischer realized he had overstepped his bounds when he told reporters that some in the White House were noting their comments and they should "watch what they say." Reporters practically leaped out of their seats.

"What did you say?" they demanded in chorus. Looking abashed, he quickly left the podium.

Sometimes he was even laughed off the podium, but not often. Fleischer was articulate and had perfected the proverbial game of ducking and dodging when questions became too tough.

In the long run-up to the invasion of Iraq on March 19, 2003, Fleischer intoned repeatedly from the podium "9/11–Saddam Hussein," a significant staple dating back to World War II. Repetition is the key marker of falsehoods.

For months, Fleischer railed against Saddam Hussein's "weapons of mass destruction" following the lead of President Bush, Vice President Dick Cheney, and National Security Adviser Condoleezza Rice. Shameless, deliberate misinformation was dispensed day after day to the American people that led to a war that Bush had wanted since the day he entered the White House.

In the epilogue to his book *Taking Heat,* Fleischer confessed casually, "We never did find weapons of mass destruction in Iraq. Although we found old artillery shells with traces of sarin gas and other chemicals, we have yet to discover any of the chemical or biological stockpiles we thought we would discover there. Yet, President Bush still won reelection."

Two American task forces, under David Kay and later Charles Duelfer, spent millions of dollars and months in Iraq and found no unconventional weapons. Their findings verified what the United Nations inspectors, headed by Hans Blix, had tried in vain to convey to the world.

"I said from the White House podium on many occasions that we knew Saddam Hussein possessed chemical weapons. I said we knew Saddam possessed biological weapons," Fleischer continued in his book.

Any remorse at the falsehoods? Hell, no. After blaming faulty intelligence and some other world leaders who thought Iraq possessed the doomsday weapons, Fleischer said, "The Bush administration may have been wrong about Saddam's capabilities, but we weren't wrong about his intentions."

Mind reader Fleischer said that Saddam was simply "biding his time" before confronting the West and Israel with the deadly weapons. Nice going, Ari. It certainly set the tone for press secretaries anointed to warm up the crowd for war.

Fleischer and McClellan obviously did not see themselves as public servants. Nor did they aspire to such a delusion. McClellan was unflappable in defending the indefensible at times. I am, however, critical of the media for taking too long to challenge the administration on the war, to ask the tough questions, to stop accepting at face value the administration's stands on war justification, human rights, and international cooperation, including violations of the Geneva Convention.

But, then, in bashing the press, I come down even harder on Congress—the people's representatives—who cared more about reelection than opposing the madness of an unprovoked war.

All this would be sophistry if it did not carry such a terrible human price. To dismiss months of deception with Fleischer's explanation is disgraceful.

There were other press secretaries and other spokespersons. I have mentioned only a few who stand out in my mind, for better or worse. Many of their names became household words, but I doubt few were able to fold their tents and silently steal away without feeling that somewhere along the way they could have done better.

CHAPTER 5

SPINNING THE NEWS

I don't believe there has been any administration that has not tried to manage, control, censor, or "spin" the news from the White House. It goes with the turf and reflects the efforts of image-makers to always try to put the president's best foot forward. How the press reacts to the manipulation is another story.

As stated earlier, the relationship between the government and the press is adversarial—and may it ever be so. That does not mean we lack respect for those in public service, but the public can only be protected from abuse by those who control the levers of government when there is an objective observer watching, checking, and critiquing those who govern us. It is natural for any administration to try to control all aspects of government information—and to hope that reporters take their press releases as gospel, without question. Fortunately, that is not the way it works. The government can present its position, but then it is up to the reporter to find the *real* story.

Reporters have a right and a duty to suspect the motives of officials, especially those who want to perpetuate themselves in office, as presidents do. Every administration has found that the media see themselves as watchdogs, not lapdogs. Unfortunately, the events surrounding 9/11 and the war in Iraq subdued the natural skepticism of the press, due in part to its fear of being castigated as "unpatriotic."

But there are still some reporters around to challenge and buck the White House's relentless 24-7 attempt to manage and control the news, standard operating procedure in the Bush-2 administration. Some reporters finally learned to push back. In fairness, the Bush administration, on the tailwind of security threats, did not invent "managed news." But it has tried to perfect it—to the detriment of the public good.

Of course, the interpretation of news context, emphasis, and forthrightness may vary from individual to individual. In essence, everyone, in every aspect of life, manages the news. President Ford's first press secretary, Jerry terHorst, said, "Management of the news is just something we all do every day." If the ethics of corporations are questioned in their presentation of product information to the public, then certainly the president of the United States cannot object if he is held accountable to the highest standards of scrutiny.

The term *managed news* is relatively new, having been coined during the administration of John F. Kennedy. Its recent application, however, is not totally appropriate, because the news has been managed by presidents since the foundation of the republic. The classic illustration of brute management of the news was the passage of the Alien and Sedition Acts in 1798, at the request of President John Adams. The acts, passed by the Federalist Congress just seven years after the adoption of the First Amendment, were designed to "manage" the opposition to war policy. But in the 1964 case *New York Times v. Sullivan,* Justice William J. Brennan said the Sedition Act was unconstitutional since "the central meaning of the First Amendment" was the right to criticize government officials.

In 1795, President George Washington refused to discuss in public special envoy John Jay's treaty that was negotiated with Great Britain. Instead of providing the Treaty to the press for public discussion, Washington presented it in a closed session to the U.S. Senate. Ultimately, this attempt at secrecy failed when Senator Stevens Thomson Mason sent a copy of it to the *Philadelphia Aurora*—which published it immediately—making the senator one of the first official "leakers." Even the Great Liberator, President Abraham Lincoln, managed the news, going beyond the restrictions of Civil War censorship. Lincoln's advisers used touch-up techniques to shorten his neck and remove scar marks from his face in pictures sent around the country to the newspapers. In the 1930s and '40s, President Franklin D. Roosevelt, afflicted with polio, was never photographed on crutches or in a wheelchair. The photographers were obeying the wishes of the White House.

While all the presidents have, in one way or another, managed the news, the effect of "news management" upon modern decision-making is more pervasive. This is the result of many different factors that include, but are certainly not limited to, increasingly sophisticated mass communications technology, larger presidential staffs, more aggressive circulation and ratings wars, the rise of advocacy journalism, sophisticated pollsters, the extremely complex issues that face the country, a far larger federal bureaucracy, and bitter partisan division. Whatever its causes, it is reason for alarm. As former Senator Mark Hatfield observed, "Every time truth is distorted or denied us, we are denied a bit of our liberty."

In spite of attempts at news management, the American public wants and needs the unencumbered facts. The population of the country is well educated and I believe capable of responding intelligently when given the basis upon which it should make a decision in a truthful and forthright way.

The modern presidency, however, seems especially to believe that trust cannot be placed in the hands of its citizens by giving them objective facts. Thus, "managed news" has become an art form—the symbol of the "imperial presidency"—and results in attempts to present all information in a controlled environment. Its spokespeople presume that its audience has no ability to assimilate, correlate, or draw proper conclusions alone and must be controlled by a prestructured format. This results in "spin," and the less access reporters have, the more government controls the message.

Ordinarily, there is less managed news at the outset of a presidential administration. This "honeymoon period" is characterized by cooperation between the president, his staff, and the press. Generally, the media report the chief executive's plans for the organization of his administration and the appointment of top officials. Because not many policies have been formulated at this point, the press does not have much to analyze, and the president need not worry about criticism. As a result, the president is anxious to simply "make news," and he generally allows the First Amendment to stand unencumbered as the basis for free and informed opinion. However, this initial period comes to a halt when the president and his administration formulate policies that are open to analysis and criticism. Then the president begins to attempt to manage the news—and the conflict unfolds.

While every presidential administration has managed the news in different and unique ways, which have been specifically suited to the particular circumstances and issues of its time, every modern presidential administration has utilized many of the same techniques. The first, and perhaps easiest, way to manage the news is simply to deny reporters access to information or an event. For instance, in the Spanish-American War, the Vietnam War, and the invasion of Grenada, press accreditation was taken away in an effort to keep the media at a distance from the crisis at hand. During the 2003 Iraq War, the United States, through the guise of the Iraqi officials, banned Aljazeera, the Qatar-based TV network, from covering it.

Second, the president and his staff can harass reporters so that they will present the news in a manner acceptable to the chief executive. This can be accomplished through any number of different means. One is to create an environment that makes the gathering of information almost impossible. An extreme example of such interference was the brutal police action in Chicago against the antiwar protesters during the 1968 Democratic National Convention. The police, on orders from Mayor Richard Daley, teargassed demonstrators and reporters who had assembled. The Vietnam War protesters wanted to send a message to the Democrats and presidential candidate Hubert Humphrey, but the presence of twelve thousand police officers and the Illinois National Guard resulted in a bloody riot. Over five hundred people were arrested, and more than two hundred were injured.

Other methods of media harassment commonly used by the White House are threatening to take away press privileges, such as accompanying the president on Air Force One, and attempting to have reporters reprimanded by their publishers if they write a piece that the president disapproves of. President Kennedy once had the chairman of the Joint Chiefs of Staff complain directly to David Halberstam's publisher about a Vietnam story that Kennedy found objectionable. Press secretaries are more flagrant in this kind of intimidation. But great publishers and editors listen politely, check the facts, and stand by reporters when they are right.

Third, members of a presidential administration often tell the media "white lies" in an attempt to control news. This usually means giving the press only part of the entire story, although sometimes it involves telling actual lies. One of the well-known examples of this took place under the Eisenhower administration with the U-2 incident. In this case, the president and his top advisers attempted to give a false story to the media to cover up that a U.S. spy plane had been brought down by a surface-to-air missile fired by the Soviet Union. However, the U.S. government's cover story backfired when Soviet Premier Khrushchev produced the plane and the plane's pilot. After the incident was over, President Eisenhower's press secretary, James Hagerty, said, "If there was any mistake in the U-2 affair, it was that we moved too fast on our cover story." But the mistake was to have lied in the first place, especially when caught red-handed.

Fourth, the president and his staff can try to control the news in such a way as to create favorable publicity for the White House and its policies. Typically this is accomplished by managing government leaks. This can entail one of two types of control: the White House can purposely leak information to the press, or the White House can attempt to prevent members of the staff from leaking any information at all. President George W. Bush goes ballistic over leaks—and has laid down the law to his cowed staff. The first type of control is often used as a "trial balloon" to see how a particular policy will "fly," while the second is simply another method of denying the media information that may prove unfavorable to the president, his policies, or members of his staff.

Fifth, White House news management can be accomplished through the timing of news and the way in which it is disseminated. These elements include the use of press releases, the daily briefing, and the presidential news conference. Press releases can be spaced so as to emphasize one story or another, or to divert attention from controversial stories. For example, President Nixon often used press releases to create news as a diversion from his involvement in the Watergate scandal. At daily briefings the press is allowed to ask the presidential press secretary questions, but White House officials still control the issues and when they will be discussed—and the time at which the briefings will (or will not) take place.

And while the presidential press conference appears to be an open forum for questions, it is, in reality, controlled by the White House. It is staged by the White House, and the president's answers are prepared, scrutinized, and rehearsed before the actual event ever begins.

President Reagan would bone up at the presidential retreat, Camp David, for prime-time news conferences. All presidents rehearse for the appearances in various ways. Their press secretaries call around the government departments to cover all bases and make sure the president is not taken off guard by a hardball question.

In addition, the president decides when to hold or not hold a press conference, and he often avoids calling on reporters known for tough questions. The timing of a news conference usually depends on the need for a presidential statement to the nation— or whether there is good news to report. If a president goes too long without a news conference, the pressure builds up from the press corps to hold one.

This type of management was especially prevalent during the Kennedy, Johnson, and Reagan administrations, and the George W. Bush White House has raised it to new levels—with Bush appearing at press conferences with a prepared list of reporters to call on. Also, many administrations hold major "bad" news announcements until after the evening news broadcasts on Friday or until after the stock market closes.

Thus, while all modern presidents have clearly managed the news to some extent, a look back at the earlier modern presidencies under my watch may shed some light on how we got to where we are today. It seems that each successive administration is more and more willing to manage the news because during the 1980s the press defaulted on its responsibility by letting the Reagan administration decide what actually was news.

It is difficult to know why the long-standing practice of news management was first formally recognized by members of the press corps and the American people during John F. Kennedy's term. However, it is not difficult to tell why accusations of controlled news became commonplace throughout his administration.

Varied practices made President Kennedy an artful news manager. First, when his press secretary, Pierre Salinger, came to the White House, he implemented several different policies with regard to the media. Among the many changes instituted was a requirement that all "important" news be coordinated by the

White House. This resulted from the previously mentioned handling of the U-2 incident, during which the United States was caught lying when four separate administration stories appeared just hours after Francis Gary Powers's plane had been shot down. In an effort to avoid such a catastrophe, Salinger required that all statements of national and international import from all the departments of the executive branch be cleared by a coordinating committee in the White House. While cries of censorship were heard from members of the press, Salinger claimed that this was, in reality, not a new procedure. He held that James Hagerty, and all previous press secretaries, had an "invisible" control over departmental press officers, and that he had only formalized the procedure. However, the point is that Salinger did formalize this type of control.

Another area in which Kennedy often practiced news management is, perhaps, even more extreme. Because President Kennedy thought that it was important for the government to speak with one voice, the chief executive demanded that all speeches be cleared by him. In addition, if Kennedy considered something to be especially important or sensitive, he would attempt to require that everyone refer all reporters' questions directly to the White House.

Kennedy deliberately divulged "secrets" to specific reporters, knowing full well that his planted story would get into the papers. At times, this practice became almost as common as the formal statements that the president made periodically to the public and the White House press corps. Many of these "private" sessions that Kennedy held took the form of friendly gatherings in which the president was simply seeking the companionship of news reporters. Because of this congenial relationship, Kennedy's job as a news manager was made somewhat easier.

However, another method of control points to the fact that Kennedy did not always have a friendly relationship with all members of the press. He often reprimanded reporters for stories that he interpreted as unfair or unfavorable. While he sometimes took it upon himself to inform the reporter in question through a note or phone call, more often than not he had a member of his White House staff chastise the correspondent in his behalf. But Kennedy's gibes against the press were mild rebukes compared to those of Franklin D. Roosevelt, who once told a reporter to go stand in the corner and put on a dunce cap.

President Kennedy also attempted to prevent the publication of certain information. A presidential request was typically made for the "security" of the country and often included an explanation of how early publication of the information would harm the careful planning of a particular event. National security has almost always been evoked to explain why news management is necessary.

Finally, Kennedy engaged in what might be called public relations. He constantly tried to stress the good news of his administration over the bad news. By emphasizing the White House's achievements, the president was often able to justify actions that might otherwise have come into question. At times, the Kennedy administration even went so far as to attempt to create "good" news.

On one occasion, the president discovered a letter to the 1908 commandant of the Marine Corps from President Theodore Roosevelt. In the letter, Roosevelt said that officers in the marines should periodically hike fifty miles as a demonstration of their fitness, and that members of the White House staff would be asked to do the same. Kennedy liked the idea so well that he sent a copy of Roosevelt's letter to the current Marine Corps commandant with the following memo attached: "Why don't you send this back to me as your own discovery? You might want to add a comment that today's Marine Corps officers are just as fit as those of 1908, and are willing to prove it. I, in turn, will ask Mr. Salinger for a report on the fitness of the White House staff."

The commandant responded by informing President Kennedy that a group of leathernecks from Camp Lejeune would be asked to hike fifty miles the next week. Kennedy then passed the response on to Salinger to let the press know of the event. Salinger said of the president's actions, "Now I have always denied accusations of news management against the Kennedy administration, but in this one instance the president was clearly guilty."

However, it is not so much in the day-to-day operations of the White House that the Kennedy administration is remembered for its management of the news, but rather in its handling of major foreign policy catastrophes.

The Bay of Pigs incident took place in the first part of Kennedy's administration. A group of Cuban exiles, trained by the CIA and backed by the U.S. government, invaded Cuba hoping to overthrow the Communist government of Fidel Castro. However, the invasion was a disaster, and over one thousand exiles were captured. While preliminary plans for the invasion were being made, there were stories in the papers hinting that some type of an incursion in Cuba would be made.

President Kennedy was aware that information had been leaked, but he still demanded absolute secrecy in the interest of national security. As mentioned earlier, even Pierre Salinger was unaware of the projected invasion (other than what he read in the papers) until he got a phone call from the president. Kennedy told his press secretary to stay close to home for the evening, and if questioned by reporters about a military operation in the Caribbean to say that he only knew what he had read.

Salinger received a second phone call at 3:30 a.m. The army duty officer in the White House situation room told him that units of an exile brigade were invading Cuba, but to keep it from appearing as though anything unusual was taking place, Salinger was to arrive at the White House at his normal time. Neither Salinger nor any other information officer in the government knew anything about the Cuban situation until these two phone calls.

This was to avoid confrontation with the press. After all, if

Salinger did not know about the covert operations, he would not be forced to answer reporters' questions about the situation at briefings, and he would not be placed in an awkward position where he might have to lie to the press.

Following a pre-invasion air strike against Castro's Cuba, Salinger told reporters at a briefing that the only information the White House had obtained came from wire pieces they had read. This, of course, was not true. Even during the actual invasion, a Kennedy spokesman refused to be honest with reporters, telling them that five thousand troops were sent. In reality, only a thousand troops had been sent. It would appear that the president was trying to use the press to get people to support a large invasion force. Then, when the troops did not succeed, White House officials told the media that just a few hundred troops had been sent, and that their role was not to invade, but rather to bring supplies to anti-Castro forces.

Following the Bay of Pigs incident, President Kennedy's relationship with the press began to disintegrate significantly. The issue, of course, was freedom of information, and accusations of censorship and news management became commonplace. From the earliest days of his administration, Kennedy acknowledged that he would be drawing certain lines. Just five days after JFK took office, he spoke to the National Press Club. This speech set off the first debate surrounding freedom of information when he said that the Kennedy administration would "have an open information policy within the confines of the national security." The important point, in the eyes of the hundreds of reporters present, was that Kennedy had already qualified what was meant by "an open information policy." Even after the Bay of Pigs was over, Kennedy still used this national security qualifier.

One week following the invasion, Kennedy held a press conference at which he said he did not wish to answer any questions regarding the incident since it would not serve any "useful national purpose." Once again, the president and the press collided head-on. In an attempt to explain his reasoning, Kennedy then made a speech to the American Newspaper Publishers Association, stressing the need for cooperation when national security is involved. However, the president's speech backfired, and the press interpreted Kennedy's words as a reprimand for pre-invasion reports, and as a suggestion of possible future censorship.

One final attempt was made by the president to sway the press to his position following the Bay of Pigs. He invited seven top newspaper executives to meet with him in the White House. The meeting, like all of the previous meetings and speeches, was not successful in reconciling the differences. Kennedy asked for self-restraint on the part of the press; the press asked for an end to censorship on the part of the president; and the news-management controversy continued.

Before the Bay of Pigs operation, when Kennedy found out that the *Miami Herald* and the *New York Times* were aware of it, he personally asked them to hold off publication. They did. After the failed invasion when Kennedy realized its folly, he said he wished he had not intervened with the newspapers and could thus have learned it would be a disastrous move.

However, the Kennedy administration's education in this regard was apparently short-lived. The next year, in 1962, President Kennedy managed the news in another situation in much the same way. U.S. intelligence found that the Soviet Union had positioned offensive missiles in Cuba that had the ability to hit various targets in the United States. President Kennedy immediately insisted that the missiles had to be removed from Cuba. On October 22, 1962, the president told the country that a blockade of Cuba by U.S. ships was being put in effect to prevent the delivery of any more missiles. Kennedy also warned that the United States would take drastic action if the missiles already placed in Cuba were not removed forthwith. In the end, the Soviet Union agreed to remove the missiles, rather than face nuclear war.

Just as the Kennedy administration had made a concerted

effort to manage the news during the Bay of Pigs, it placed all kinds of controls on the flow of information to the White House press corps and the American people during the Cuban missile crisis. Throughout the early stages of this head-on confrontation with the Soviet Union, President Kennedy cut short a trip to Chicago and flew back to Washington. Salinger told the press that Kennedy was returning to the White House because he had a "cold."

This was misinformation to conceal why the president was not going on his scheduled midterm campaign tour of the country. Reporters soon found out that the real reason he was at the White House was to get the latest information on the Cuban weapons buildup. Kennedy also directed that the White House keep a lid on all news releases.

Beyond this, Kennedy imposed restrictions on State Department and Pentagon media contacts and required White House aides to clear any contact with the press through Pierre Salinger beforehand. Then, following an interview with a member of the media, the White House staffer was required to turn in a written report on those areas that were discussed with reporters.

Although the term *news management* originated in the Kennedy era, the trend has only gotten worse with each successive administration. During the Johnson years this phenomenon led to the all-encompassing term *credibility gap.* In fact, this "credibility gap" was cited by Johnson himself as the area of his administration's biggest failure. Johnson was prone to overreact when charged with a credibility gap; he preferred to turn the tables and made frequent references to "press credibility." This included pointing out everything from typographical errors to what he saw as misinterpretations.

I don't know how many times I heard Johnson complain, "You all have the First Amendment as if it was a special weapon against presidents." Come to think of it—it is. One of the reasons this situation developed was because Johnson always believed the press was plotting against him. One obvious result was the abolition of the press pool that traveled with the president on Air Force One. This pool comprised a correspondent from both wire services, a correspondent from each of the networks, and a correspondent chosen from the "general" reporters covering the trip. The purpose of the pool was to be certain of qualified press coverage in case of emergency.

However, Johnson believed the reporters were there as "spies" trying to pry into his secrets. Initially, Johnson tried to control the spies by sitting with them during presidential trips. But, when this approach did not succeed in softening up reporters, the president moved to have the press pool abolished. He claimed that the concept of the pool had been initiated by Pierre Salinger in the previous administration, and this White House was simply going to change the way in which the chief executive was covered. George Reedy, President Johnson's press secretary at the time, suggested that the press pool had become an "accepted institution" since it had been created by James Hagerty under the Eisenhower administration. Nonetheless, Johnson went ahead with his plans and did away with the pool. This technique not only managed the news, but also basically eliminated it.

It did not last long—and the pool was soon back on the presidential plane. That's the way it was with Johnson's piques—they were short-lived.

In addition to temporarily abolishing the press pool, President Johnson often had his press secretary or a White House assistant call reporters and their publishers to grumble about stories that he did not like. He claimed that he enjoyed this approach because "at least those bastards know what I think of them." However, the news management aspect that especially irritated reporters during the Johnson era was the president's habit of withholding upcoming travel plans until the last minute—often leaving reporters scrambling to catch up, say good-bye to their loved ones, and pack a bag.

Another source of irritation with Johnson was his timing of the release of information. He usually announced good news when it would get prime-time television coverage and buried bad news. On one occasion, his administration requested that Congress schedule the State of the Union address for nine in the evening, instead of the usual hour of noon. This way Johnson could appear during prime time. In fact, the medium of television encouraged the Johnson White House to work hard at the optimum timing for the release of information or for events.

When controlling timing was ineffective, the Johnson administration simply avoided reporters' questions. This meant keeping certain members of the White House staff away from inquisitive reporters, and referring difficult questions to other government agencies or departments. During George Christian's term as press secretary, he openly admitted to avoiding inquiries about the crew of the hijacked USS *Pueblo.* "For nearly a year, it was shameful the way I avoided answering questions about the crew of the *Pueblo,* referring everything to the State Department. The intent was to keep everything on the subject away from the White House." The *Pueblo* was a U.S. intelligence ship grabbed by the North Koreans in the Sea of Japan whose crew was held for eleven months. But after stories of the capture, they were forgotten men until finally released. President Johnson was not taunted every day about the failure to rescue the *Pueblo* crew as the benighted Jimmy Carter was during the 444-day Iranian hostage crisis.

President Johnson also was known for granting favors to reporters writing "good stories." However, news management through manipulation of reporters that one has befriended can also backfire. One example involved President Johnson's longtime friend, columnist William S. White. During the Johnson era, White's circulation dropped significantly because of his friendship with the president. In addition, White's politics were more conservative than Johnson's. Yet White could not write as "forcefully" as he wanted without embarrassing the White House since his words were assumed to have come directly from the president. In addition, by befriending only certain reporters,

Johnson automatically created enemies in those not given this favoritism.

Another instance also resulted in trouble. This incident took place at the president's ranch. Following Johnson's heart attack in 1955, the doctor suggested that he walk a half mile each day, and he followed his doctor's orders diligently. It just so happened that his cousin Oriole's front door was a half mile from the front of his ranch, so every night LBJ would visit Cousin Oriole, an elderly woman who lived "frontier style." Based on the "fact" that the old woman was almost entirely deaf (she was only somewhat deaf), Johnson found it necessary to pound on Cousin Oriole's door, making as much commotion as possible.

Eventually, after sufficient time, Cousin Oriole would pad to the door in bare feet. She always acted annoyed but, in reality, enjoyed the attention. For the next twenty minutes, all those accompanying the president on his walk would listen while Johnson asked Cousin Oriole about the sheep that the elderly woman took care of for the president, though Cousin Oriole typically heard the word *sheep* as *sleep.*

One night Johnson allowed the press to accompany him on this nightly ritual to Cousin Oriole's and I wrote a piece on it. George Reedy, the press secretary, said I had "captured the essence of the occasion—the smell of the frontier, Cousin Oriole's fierce independence, Johnson's rough, but somehow tender, sensitivity to the loneliness of an elderly widow." And Reedy also believed the piece "spelled out votes by the millions" for the president. However, Johnson did not think so. He resented what he thought was an attempt to harm the Johnson family image, so he decided to "punish" me. He stopped "wining and dining" me. He no longer invited me to the ranch, and he no longer considered me the friend he once did. I was in the deep freeze for a while.

More than any other single issue in the Johnson White House, the Vietnam War caused the credibility gap to widen. George Christian claimed that "after the Vietnam effort began to decay, some in the news media could find little that was 'right' with Johnson."

For instance, the Pentagon Papers revealed that President Johnson had changed the course in Vietnam on April 1, 1965, from defense to active combat. But, at a news conference that very week, the president told reporters, "I know of no far-reaching strategy that is being suggested or promulgated" to commit U.S. troops to fighting on the ground in Vietnam. Here were shades of the dissembling we were to hear later from Bush-1 as he planned the first Gulf War and Bush-2 on the way to the Iraq War.

In a similar matter, President Johnson was asked at a March 9, 1967, press conference if he was looking for a successor for Ambassador Henry Cabot Lodge at Saigon. He said, "No, there is no truth that I am looking for a successor," and that a date had not been set for Lodge to leave. In less than a week, Ellsworth Bunker replaced Lodge. When LBJ's press secretary was asked about the president's answer earlier that week, the press was told that Johnson's answer was "absolutely accurate." The press secretary explained that the president had already chosen Lodge's successor by March 9, so he was not looking for a successor anymore.

Thus, the credibility gap continued to widen, and the practice of news management continued throughout the entire Johnson era—and the following administrations. Even the Freedom of Information Act of 1967 did not significantly curtail news management. However, this act was an important step in assisting the free flow of information. As Attorney General Ramsey Clark said, "If government is to be truly of, by, and for the people, the people must know in detail the activities of government. Nothing so diminishes democracy as secrecy. . . . Never was it more important than in our times of mass society, when government affects each individual in so many ways, that the right of the people to know the actions of their government be secure."

Unlike the previous two administrations, the Nixon White

House began their policy of news management from the outset. In fact, the news was even managed by Richard Nixon and his staff throughout the 1968 presidential campaign. One of Nixon's primary campaign tools was the use of taped television segments that could be produced in the controlled environment of a TV studio, and no reporters were allowed at any of the presidential candidate's tapings. This resulted in reporters being denied the ability to cover the "real" campaign, while Nixon was allowed to hide in the security of a studio. Nixon believed that the public would rely on the television version of Richard Nixon, instead of a secondhand version the press might present.

Throughout that campaign in 1968, in which Vice President Hubert Humphrey tried in vain to extricate himself from LBJ's failed Vietnam policies, Nixon said he had a "secret" plan to end the war. Reporters never got to ask him what it was. Not until he got into the White House did we learn it was Vietnamization—to try to turn the fighting over to the South Vietnamese.

One example of Nixon controlling the story during the campaign was when David Broder of the *Washington Post* predicted in an article that Spiro Agnew might be chosen as the presidential candidate's running mate. While other members of the press thought Broder had some sort of amazing power of prediction, it was later learned that the story was a plant that had come directly from Nixon. The plant was a "trial balloon" to get the reaction of the press and the public.

By the time he got to the White House, Nixon had a well-worn chip on his shoulder against the press. In 1969, he designated Vice President Spiro Agnew to kick off an antimedia campaign accusing reporters of bias and instant analysis. Richard Nixon's efforts at news management only increased with time, and as the 1972 election approached, members of the president's staff became more and more brazen. For instance, on one occasion the White House blocked a television crew from filming anti–Vietnam War demonstrators on the campaign trail. Instead, at the same campaign stop, Nixon ordered the crew to film some schoolchildren who were shouting, "Four more years."

During Nixon's White House years, news management was made into a new science, using any number of nefarious techniques. For instance, President Nixon had the telephones of "offending" reporters wiretapped; the vice president spoke across the country about "disloyal" reporters; the Department of Justice attempted to subpoena reporters' notes; and a White House aide, acting under instructions from the president, alerted the television networks that they faced the possibility of antitrust lawsuits if they did not let more conservatives on the networks.

The White House was so overtly concerned with news management that Henry Kissinger was only allowed to speak on "background" at press conferences and was never allowed to appear on television until the end of Nixon's first term. Apparently, Nixon's public relations staff worried that Kissinger's foreign accent might not be acceptable to Middle America. When Kissinger was finally given permission to speak "on the record," no audio recording was allowed—only video. As it was, Kissinger could upstage Nixon with his know-it-all air and outsize ego.

In many ways, even the news management techniques employed by previous administrations were taken to new extremes in the Nixon White House. For instance, on one occasion, Daniel Schorr did a "critical" piece on the Nixon administration for CBS. The White House responded by having Schorr investigated by the FBI on the false pretense that he was a candidate for a government post. The harassment was, undoubtedly, a signal to Schorr that the president did not want any further critical pieces broadcast.

When Jules Witcover wrote a book about Nixon's 1968 campaign called *The Resurrection of Richard Nixon,* which was not especially complimentary to the president, a similar type of intimidation occurred. In this case, the White House called many of Witcover's known sources and told them not to talk to him anymore. Then, when Witcover went on a talk show to defend his book, the White House ordered the IRS to investigate the author.

In addition, Nixon's press secretary, Ron Ziegler, often used what has been referred to as the "squeeze play" in his attempts to use timing to control the flow of information. A typical scenario of this might proceed as follows: Ziegler would schedule a briefing for eleven, but would not show up until eleven thirty or so. This meant that the briefing could only last fifteen minutes, because noon was the deadline for many reporters, and they needed time to transpose their information into a story. By starting the briefing late and limiting its time, Ziegler made sure that reporters did not have time to dwell too long on any one topic—such as Watergate.

Two outstanding illustrations of news management were the Vietnam War generally, which is, perhaps, best exemplified by the handling of the Pentagon Papers, and the well-known Watergate scandal. Nixon wrote in his book *Leaders,* "Until human nature itself changes, people will leak information in order to accomplish their ends. In most cases those ends are individual self-advancement. In some cases, however, people are concerned about the dangers of a policy they consider to be wrong."

While Nixon's statement was not made specifically in reference to the Pentagon Papers, the former president was dealing with his general thoughts regarding the leaking of information about the Vietnam War. Nixon consistently reiterated his negative view, and his belief that these leaks "jeopardized our negotiations and, rather than shortening the war, prolonged it." However, as Arthur Schlesinger Jr. writes, "In recent American experience the misfortunes averted by publicity were clearer than the losses entailed. After all the years of the American obsession with secrecy, could anyone name a case where a leak did serious damage to the national security? Conceivably the nation might have been better off had there been more rather than fewer leaks."

Of course, national security was not the only basis upon which the Nixon administration claimed a "right" to manage the news. The most blatant example of Nixon's claim of "executive privilege" and his management of the news took place in the events surrounding the Watergate affair. From the outset, as soon as reporters began looking into the president's involvement, the White House openly showed its unhappiness.

For instance, when the *Washington Post* went ahead with its investigation into Watergate, people tied to the 1972 campaign challenged the license renewals of two television stations in Florida that were owned by the *Post*. This, in turn, caused the value of *Washington Post* stock to fall by 25 percent in one night.

The TV harassment was only the beginning. It is not necessary to describe in morbid detail the scenario of fraud, deception, and deceit because everyone who was around at that time has these events burned into his or her memory. In this context, it is interesting to note that the Watergate fiasco somewhat began as a news management problem. Once the circumscribing and covering up of this event began, it started to unravel, and "all the president's men"—and even the president—ultimately fell.

Perhaps Watergate is the best proof that the journalist's abhorrence of managed news is valid. When the principle of managed news is accepted, we then leave the boundaries of that management solely to the discretion of that president. And it should never be in the hands of one man—that would give him dictatorial powers and presidential control over government news.

For five whole months during the height of the Watergate trauma, Nixon held no news conferences. In addition, the presidential press secretary, Ron Ziegler, did not meet with the press for more than a year, and his duties were taken over by an underling, Deputy Press Secretary Gerald Warren. In addition, even Ziegler was being denied access to the president during this time. Jerry terHorst, then White House correspondent for the *Detroit News*, explained, "There were days that went by when Ron Ziegler would not even see Richard Nixon." TerHorst tells a story about a time when Ziegler complained to one of the president's top confidants about never seeing the president. The press secretary was taken by the arm, led to the Oval Office, instructed to look inside, and told, "Now you've seen the president for the day."

There was an absolute refusal to provide information. Perhaps this is best exemplified when the president, under a claim of executive privilege, attempted to deny the special prosecutor access to the Watergate tapes. In writing for an 8–0 Supreme Court majority in the Watergate tapes case, Chief Justice Warren Burger said, "No case of the Court, however, has extended this high degree of deference to a President's generalized interest in confidentiality. Nowhere in the Constitution, as we have noted earlier, is there any explicit reference to a privilege of confidentiality."

Thus, it is clear that the Nixon administration's attempts to control the news surrounding Watergate went far beyond previous news management attempts. It takes no great thought to realize that Watergate was not some simple press agent's fumbling attempt to manipulate the press. Rather, the criminal convictions and the resignation of the president of the United States illustrate that Watergate was different in kind, and we do a disservice to compare Richard Nixon to other presidents. It was really his abuse of government power that led to his demise. The White House's accountability reached the lowest point I've seen in my years of covering the presidents. It was not even managed news. It was a total blackout. We didn't know what to believe anymore from the people who were beleaguered. Some thirty aides were indicted or went to prison.

In fact, Nixon felt so absolutely desperate that on one of his final days at the White House he actually had the press locked inside the pressroom with Secret Service agents posted as guards. This was the only way he felt he could take one last walk around the White House without having to contend with the press—this was the ultimate in news management.

The deteriorating relationship between the White House and the press was obvious to President Gerald Ford when he assumed office after the divisive Watergate years. In his first public exchange as president, Ford pronounced his intentions to stick to a policy of "openness and candor" with the American people. Subsequently, the president told his cabinet members to remain open to the public and the press.

Despite these early proclamations by President Ford, and despite the White House's instincts to distance themselves from the dark days of the Nixon era, the news management soon began. Probably the most blatant example of controlling information came shortly after Ford appointed his first press secretary, Jerald terHorst, and told him he was not even considering a pardon for Nixon. When, on September 8, 1974, barely a month after taking office, Ford issued a "full, free, and absolute pardon" to Richard Nixon, Jerry terHorst resigned. He became a hero to reporters for his integrity.

Jimmy Carter campaigned as an "outsider" to Washington and, therefore, arrived at the White House as an outsider. This mentality led to some antipathy toward the established press corps, which, in turn, often led to poor relations with the White House press. In fact, Carter's press secretary, Jody Powell, has written, "We failed to appreciate until too late the repercussions of our failure to socialize in the traditional Washington manner. We missed an opportunity to get to know Washington better." He went on to say, "We failed to establish personal relationships with individuals who could have been helpful to us professionally." So, at the outset, Carter and his staff ran an "open" White House with little effort to spin the news.

Despite initially refraining from overt control over the press, eventually, like all other presidents in crisis mode, Carter succumbed to news management tactics. With inflation out of control and an energy crisis at hand, the White House was then hit with the Iranian hostage crisis. Everything was downhill for Carter from then on.

The overthrow of the Shah of Iran by an Islamic revolutionary group meant eroded relations between the United States and Iran. On November 4, 1979, in response to the admission of the former shah to the United States for cancer treatment, Iranian combatants stampeded the U.S. embassy in Tehran, taking approximately seventy of its employees hostage. The hostages were held for a total of 444 days.

Because of Carter's desire to bring the hostages home safely, a rescue mission was attempted on April 24, 1980. Two days before its failure, press secretary Jody Powell told the *Los Angeles Times* that such a mission would not be logical—the obvious implication being that there was not going to be any rescue endeavor. So much for the Carter White House's policy of open government.

But television commentators and anchormen were relentless in citing how many days it had been that the hostages were being held, fueling the perception that Carter was a weak president. In truth, he brought the hostages back alive. But President Reagan got the credit, because the Iranians waited until the day Reagan was sworn in to release them.

Ronald Reagan's acting press secretary, Larry Speakes, had a sign on his desk at the White House that read, "You don't tell us how to stage the news and we don't tell you how to cover it." This sign spoke volumes since Reagan was a master at controlling the news. The White House was particularly captivated by the visual images of television. Each day, the administration focused on a story and worked to get certain images related to the story on the air. Director of Communications David Gergen, on his last day at 1600 Pennsylvania Avenue in 1984, said, "The White House is like a stage." And the stage productions were produced, directed, and acted by the administration. But the master of image-making was Deputy Chief of

Staff Mike Deaver—who masterminded Reagan's public relations.

Reagan not only concerned himself with getting the proper images broadcast, but also was careful to insure that certain images were not seen on television. In October of 1983, the small island nation of Grenada had a bloody coup. The government was overthrown by hard-line Marxists—who the administration claimed threatened the region's stability. On October 25 of that year, roughly seven thousand U.S. troops invaded Grenada. The day before the invasion, Larry Speakes said the idea of an invasion was "preposterous." The White House then barred press coverage, instead providing its own videotapes to the television networks. None of the tapes showed any pictures of actual combat.

Ronald Reagan also was famous for cupping his ear when boarding Marine One on the South Lawn of the White House, claiming he could not hear our questions above the noise of the helicopter. And, beginning in 1982, it became this administration's policy that no questions were to be asked at "photo opportunities." The press would file into the Oval Office to see the president with a head of state or other visitor; the photographers would snap their pictures; and we were unceremoniously dismissed—no information exchanged. Obviously, this insured that Reagan didn't veer "off message" or disrupt the planned visual images. But once in a while we reporters were able to goad Reagan into answering our impromptu questions. His top aides would become apoplectic at the unplanned news conference.

Unlike Jimmy Carter, and to some degree Ronald Reagan, George Herbert Walker Bush came to office as the quintessential Washington insider. As a result, he liked the Washington press corps, viewing them as part of the exclusive political class. He often held spur-of-the-moment press conferences in the White House briefing room and had a certain comfort with the media covering him. At the end of the day, he frequently kibitzed with reporters and photographers and aroused good feelings between the White House and the press.

However, like all his predecessors, George Bush eventually caved to his advisers—and the news management began. The Persian Gulf War was a point in fact. In August of 1990, Iraq and Kuwait were divided over the issues of border changes and an oil field (most of which was on the Kuwait side of the border). When negotiations failed, Iraq invaded Kuwait. A coalition of thirty-four nations, led by the United States, was authorized by the United Nations to force Iraqi withdrawal from Kuwait. Much of our country was split over how far Americans should go in extricating Kuwait.

Reporters who covered the Gulf War were immediately restricted by the Department of Defense. The press pool had to be escorted by Defense Department officers, and coverage was tightly controlled. The media needed approval as to where they could go, and who they were allowed to interview. In many instances, the print media had to get clearance from the Pentagon before printing stories, and television cameras were not permitted near any of the fighting. Instead, the Bush administration put out their own videotapes for use by the TV networks, thereby controlling what was seen by the American public. And, many questions remained unanswered regarding the number of casualties in the war. But all controls fell apart at the end of the war when the defeated Iraqis came out of the trenches, hands up, and were shot at. The border between Iraq and Kuwait became a "highway of death," and the Bush White House knew the pictures would not play well with the world.

That Bush's friendly relationship with the media deteriorated after the administration's attempts at controlling the news goes without saying. Even Bush realized his troubles with the press. By the 1992 presidential campaign, the president was known to tell people about his favorite campaign-season bumper sticker. It read ANNOY THE MEDIA—REELECT BUSH.

Bill Clinton came to office as a popularly elected president, but this didn't stop the White House from worrying about controlling their message. They were particularly adept at avoiding the regular White House press corps. Clinton held numerous meetings with members of the local press and geared his dispatches to specifically targeted markets. At the same time, he realized the value of speaking directly to the American people and used the talk show circuit as a forum. However, even then the White House was careful to control the news by setting up certain "ground rules" the talk show hosts had to abide by—or the president would not appear on that program.

The best-known example of media manipulation during the Clinton era took place during the events surrounding the president's relationship with White House intern Monica Lewinsky. The blaring headlines of the time—that Clinton was having sex with Lewinsky in the White House—put the administration in full-scale crisis mode. The president and his lawyers judiciously worded a statement denying any "improper relationship"— which Clinton press secretary Mike McCurry read to the press.

The White House put into effect all of the usual tactics and circled the wagons: they sent emissaries to the talk shows, First Lady Hillary Clinton blamed "a vast right-wing conspiracy," others blamed the press, and they blatantly lied. Finally, Clinton faced the music himself. At a White House after-school-care event, Clinton told the media, "I did not have sexual relations with that woman, Miss Lewinsky." But, even the parsing of language could not kill the story—and the president's lies ultimately tarnished and overshadowed his accomplishments.

The backdrop of the origins of news management in the previous administrations I covered full-time puts into context the control of information exercised by the current administration of George W. Bush. This White House has learned their lessons well—except for the dangers inherent in such news management. In fact, even the American people understand the Bush White House's obsession with secrecy and control. In a CNN

Web site poll on May 26, 2005, the pollsters asked, "Do you think the Bush White House is trying to control the media?" An overwhelming number of respondents, 94 percent, answered yes.

In a recent column for my employer, Hearst Newspapers, I wrote a piece that gives an overview of where things currently stand in the Bush White House on news management:

> President George W. Bush has learned to use the bully pulpit that is the powerful prerogative of all presidents. But this president has tried to tweak that power in ways that expand the definition of "managed news."
>
> Let's start with his national campaign to change Social Security. As he travels around the nation to make his pitch that Social Security is in crisis, the president is limiting his congregation to screened, sanitized audiences. Why does he sermonize on the subject only to carefully selected audiences?
>
> These are people who are vetted to make sure they agree with the president's views. If they pass that test, the local Republican Party or the groups sponsoring the event then issue tickets to the so-called "town meetings" or "conversations with the president."
>
> Asked why the president speaks only to his supporters, White House press secretary Scott McClellan said Bush's intention is to "educate" the people. He probably meant "indoctrinate."
>
> Is this the president of all the people—or just some of the people who agree with him? It's bizarre. He's preaching to the choir; hardly the way to "educate" the public.
>
> Controlling his audience was a prime goal of Bush's 2004 presidential campaign, when antiwar protesters were barred from his public appearances. People who openly disagreed with him were hustled out of the hall.

We saw the same audience control when Bush spoke about Social Security. The Secret Service and the White House aides apparently spent a lot of time trying to handpick those permitted to hear him. Bush finds it hard to deal with dissent or opposition. His aides are in lockstep and never hear a discouraging word.

Bush seems satisfied that he has made Social Security a worry to people. That's the goal of his sky-is-falling campaign. But the president is not ready to handle genuine dialogue on the subject or deal with those opposed to his plan to partially privatize the government pension program. He bristles when he is opposed, so he is surrounded by "yes" men and women.

Every administration tries to manage the message that the news media convey to the public about presidential policies, problems, and successes. But the Bush White House is pioneering new methods that steer message management into outright government propaganda.

Needless to say, the Bush White House has been particularly adept at managing all of the news related to Iraq. From the "embedding" of reporters covering the war (which allows for better control over the press) to a memo from the Pentagon requesting that news organizations "not air or publish recognizable images or audio recordings that identify POWs" to scripted news conferences, this administration has denied the press and the people the right to information needed to make an informed decision.

And the information this administration dispensed about the war was too often misleading and deliberately deceptive. When Bush was leading up to the Iraq War, reporters heard daily that Saddam Hussein had an arsenal that threatened our security. Not true. He also said Iraq was the central front in the war on terrorism.

Not so. But he made it a reality by attacking the oil-rich country.

In yet another attempt to control all news related to the war, Bush-2 gave a televised, prime-time speech to the American public on the Iraq War on June 28, 2005. In the speech before seven hundred or so in the U.S. army stationed at Fort Bragg, North Carolina, the president's "stay the course" words didn't elicit much of a response from those watching their commander in chief in person—so Bush's advance team initiated applause for the televised event.

To say that the relations between any president and a free press are complex and difficult is to say the obvious. However, today, in an age of thirty-second television news clips, Madison Avenue political ads, and an ever-decreasing newspaper readership, the duties and responsibilities of a free press become paramount.

In every walk of life, individuals presume it is normal to attempt to manage the flow of information, but in an age where government is all-pervasive, where every aspect of our life is affected by that government, the public has a legitimate concern in minimizing government's ability to control what the people have a right to know. The duty of our government is to provide what our people determine they need—*not* to determine for us what we need.

CHAPTER 6

HAIL TO THE HEROIC LEAKERS AND WHISTLE-BLOWERS—AND THE JOURNALISTS WHO PROTECT THEM

So the powers that be may seek to manage the news—but they do not always succeed. This is because there are many unsung heroes and heroines who care enough about this country—and the need for truth—to leak information about wrongdoing. While it is best to name sources on a news story, oftentimes anonymity is needed to protect a source who will only speak in the strictest of confidence. As long as there are disgruntled employees, personal agendas, or a motive to further a cause, there will be anonymous sources and leaks to the media.

Presidents try to stop them unless they are doing the leaking, and corporate heads deplore them, but often the only way the public can learn the "real story" is if someone is willing to come forward under the cloak of anonymity—often at great personal risk—to use the media to expose perceived wrongdoing or simply to float a new idea or proposal.

There may be an element of self-preservation in refusing to be an identified source, but history is full of cases where wrong-doing would probably never have surfaced without information from an unnamed source. The classic case, of course, is the Watergate scandal.

In police reporting, revealing someone's identity is known as "burning a source"—but it is a rarity.

Newspapers and other publications have worked diligently to reinforce journalistic ethics standards because of miscreants like the *New York Times* reporter Jayson Blair and Jack Kelley of *USA Today.* Because they fabricated and plagiarized information and invented sources claiming they asked to remain anonymous, the use of this type of source is subject to more scrutiny.

The confidentiality and legality issue was exacerbated in 2005 when *New York Times* reporter Judith Miller protected her sources and was jailed for refusing to divulge their names to a federal court and the grand jury in the case of Valerie Plame, an outed CIA operative. Revealing the identity of a CIA undercover agent is a violation of the 1982 Intelligence Identities Protection Act. U.S. District Court Judge Thomas Hogan cited court decisions in federal cases that reporters do not have a total First Amendment protection from revealing sources, even though Ms. Miller did not actually write a story about the Plame matter for her newspaper. Hogan's ruling indicated that he felt reporters have no federal privilege—and that seems to be the trend in the ever-growing numbers of conservative courts. Thirty-one states and the District of Columbia have journalist protection laws in place to bolster the First Amendment.

Time magazine reporter Matthew Cooper's e-mails to his boss were confiscated by federal prosecutors. The documents implicated Deputy White House Chief of Staff Karl Rove as the possible "leaker" in certain aspects of the case. Cooper confirmed Rove's involvement in testimony before the grand jury looking into the Plame revelations and wrote about his testimony in *Time.*

As an example of how newspapers are working to tighten reliable-source standards, the *Los Angeles Times* (7/15/05) told its reporters and editors that anonymous sources in stories and editorials can still be used, but only as a "last resort" to convey important information that cannot be delivered by other means.

Editor John S. Carroll, now retired, in issuing the guidelines to all staff, said reporters should try to be sure that sources have a compelling reason to keep their identities secret. They should be identified in stories as precisely as possible to reveal potential biases. The guidelines say, for instance, "An advisor to Democratic members of the House Foreign Relations Committee would be a preferable identification for an unnamed source instead of simply a 'congressional source.' " In other words, since the person is identified as an adviser, a Democrat, and probably a Foreign Relations Committee staff member, a reader wouldn't have to be a rocket scientist to trace the source.

The *Los Angeles Times* guidelines are broader in scope and make fewer prohibitions than standards issued recently by other publications, but reporters and editors are warned to be careful how and where they store information on a computer that might identify an anonymous source.

It's hard to see how Washington reporters who cover the White House, the Pentagon, and other federal agencies can operate without anonymous sources, but it would be better if they did. A news story is much more effective and certainly bears a brand of accuracy when the source can be named and held accountable.

The Senate Judiciary Committee, in July 2005, held hearings on a federal bill that would shield journalists from having to disclose confidential sources, which disclosure supporters argued was impinging on the public's right to information. However, senators on both sides of the aisle said the legislation was too broadly written.

In June 2005, the Associated Press and the Associated Press Managing Editors association conducted a survey of American newspapers to learn their practices on the question of anonymous sources. It drew 419 replies, about 28 percent of the nation's 1,450 daily newspapers.

The AP said that editors at 103 papers, most of them in small and midsize markets, said they do not ever permit reporters to cite anonymous sources in their articles.

"Our policy is to get people on the record. Period," said Eileen

Lehnert, editor of Michigan's *Jackson Citizen Patriot.* "Once you operate from that standpoint, you rarely have to reconsider your position." That, of course, is the ideal, but one could also be passing up a blockbuster story with such strict standards.

Metropolitan newspapers with overseas or Washington bureaus use anonymous sources when requested, but they have instituted policies now that minimize use of quotes from unidentified persons.

Carl Lavin, deputy managing editor of the *Philadelphia Inquirer,* said that his paper discourages the use of unnamed sources, but "this needs to be balanced with the need to present vital information to the reader than cannot be obtained by any other means."

Some editors said their restrictions on unnamed sources are so great they would even have had to pass up Deep Throat in the Watergate scandal of the seventies. Others said they would use sources who declined to be identified when the information was compelling.

AP said it permits use of anonymous sources when the material, not the opinion, is vital to the news report, and when the source is considered to be reliably imparting accurate information.

Several editors told the AP they were considering applying their papers' tough policies not only to written stories, but also to stories obtained from wire services like the AP and syndication services.

It is appalling that reporters will offer anonymity to their sources even when they do not ask for it. Michael McCurry, one of former President Clinton's press secretaries, was quoted in the *Nation* magazine saying, "Unnamed sources are such a problem today in part because reporters are frequently more eager to grant anonymity than officials are to demand it.

"I have had probably thousands of conversations with reporters in twenty-five years as a press secretary," McCurry said, "and I'd say eighty percent of the time I am offered anonymity and background rather than asking for it. I rarely have to ask for it and don't ask for it because I prefer to keep on-the-record as often as I can."

There are different ways a reporter can disguise a source. The categories are background, deep background, and off-the-record. *Background* means a source can be identified as a senior administration official, or a reasonable facsimile, but without identifying him or her by name. When using information on *deep background,* a reporter simply writes the facts and gives no attribution.

During the Vietnam War, Henry Kissinger, who became secretary of state after previously holding the post of national security adviser, would often brief reporters "on background" at the White House. The backgrounder became so blatant in its overuse that the *New York Times* once printed a story attributed to a senior administration official in its prime right-hand column and published Kissinger's picture in the next column.

I used to threaten to write, "A high-ranking official in the Nixon administration, with a thick German accent, said today . . . ," but I didn't dare and I'm sure my editors would have frowned on it.

Off-the-record speaks for itself. It often provides useful background information to a reporter doing a story, but it is not for publication. A reporter's word is a solemn pledge, and when a promise is given for off-the-record, that is it. Most reporters have lived up to that trust.

In fact, at times reporters have walked out of a meeting dubbed "on background" or "off-the-record" on grounds that the terms were unacceptable and they felt they could get the information elsewhere and print it. Individualistic as they are, whenever a group of reporters decide to walk out together in protest, it's not terribly effective. One or two will be recalcitrant about acting in concert, and the backgrounder usually goes ahead on schedule under the terms laid out by the government spokesman.

President Lyndon B. Johnson used to give us news off-the-record when we knew he did not understand the term and really wanted to see his information in print, but quoting an anonymous source.

In his good book *Attack the Messenger: How Politicians Turn You Against the Media* (Rowman & Littlefield Publishers, 2005), author Craig Crawford says somewhat cynically, "Deceitfully spinning the truth is so common and expected in Washington that politicians often go off-the-record when they want to tell a reporter the truth. What does that tell you?

"Twisting the truth has gotten so perverse in Washington that few believe a quote if it is said in public. But if it is said off-the-record as an anonymous quote, it rings true. The news media is far too forgiving of politicians who want to tell the real truth anonymously. Reporters are suckers for this technique because it makes their reports seem more exotic. Sometimes . . . we have no choice. It is the only way to get the information out."

It is important to note that an anonymous source isn't necessarily a "whistle-blower." A whistle-blower is someone within an organization who witnesses behavior by colleagues that is either contrary to the mission of the organization, illegal, or threatening to the public interest and decides to speak publicly about it. Usually such people are guided by conscience and a strong moral sense.

Jeffrey Wigand is a well-known whistle-blower for his role in the Big Tobacco scandal of the nineties in which he revealed that executives of the tobacco companies knew that cigarettes were addictive and that the firms added carcinogenic ingredients to the tobacco. Wigand was fired from his job and his wife divorced him during the turmoil, but he told CBS's *60 Minutes* that he had few regrets for his brave actions.

The Enron scandal, which saw thousands of loyal employees lose their jobs and life savings, was also revealed by a sharp-eyed accountant whistle-blower. Several states and a few countries have laws on the books protecting whistle-blowers, but it is still a high-risk endeavor with few rewards except to know you did the right thing. Gratitude comes later—sometimes too late.

Whistle-blowers have often come from the ranks of the government bureaucracy and are people with the moral rectitude to protest corruption. One of the most famous is A. Ernest Fitzgerald, who served as management-systems deputy in the Office of the Assistant Secretary of the Air Force. Fitzgerald revealed the cost overruns on new cargo planes and exposed other waste in the Defense Department. Despite his dedication to saving the taxpayers' money, he was the bane of President Nixon and others in the administration. Nixon called Fitzgerald an SOB. Instead of reaping praise, he became a pariah at the Pentagon and was relegated to a small corner office and shunned. That is not an atypical fate for those who expose wrongdoing in government or in industry. Some lose their jobs or are forced to quit. In his book *Whistleblower's Handbook,* Brian Martin wrote, "When a whistleblower speaks out, the price can be formidable: loss of job, demotion, slander, ostracism, dismissal and blacklisting."

My favorite whistle-blower of recent times was Specialist Joseph Darby of Corriganville, Maryland, who at age twenty-four was a military guard at Baghdad's infamous Abu Ghraib prison. Young Darby tipped off his army superiors in January 2004 when he discovered photographs of some of his fellow members of the 372nd Military Police Company participating in the horrific abuse of the prisoners there.

Darby telephoned his mother one night and asked for her ethical advice, but he did not say what was troubling him. After talking to his mother, who told him, "The truth will make you free," he laid a disc of the photos on the bunk of an army investigator.

Darby was ostracized by his buddies, who thought he had "ratted" on them. But he was presented a special John F. Kennedy Profile in Courage Award on May 15, 2005. His brother, Larry, quoted on CBS News.com, said, "It doesn't surprise me a bit. He knows right from wrong."

"Leakers" dispense secret information to the news media as

an unnamed source. The late Pierre Salinger, press secretary to President Kennedy, used to tell of the time that Kennedy was irate over a news leak. He demanded that Salinger track down the culprit. A couple of days later, a smiling Salinger told Kennedy that he had found the leaker. "Who?" asked the president. "You," Salinger replied. It seems that Kennedy had talked too much in one of his friendly chats with a reporter.

Many press secretaries have tried to fend off presidential ire over leaks by telling the president it would be futile and self-defeating to try to find out who "blabbed," and furthermore, it would best be forgotten even if they did find out.

President Johnson was a notorious leaker himself when he was trying to plant a story with reporters. In 1965, after he'd won the presidency on his own, LBJ wanted to fire the Kennedy holdover cabinet and appoint his own team. Karl Bauman, the Associated Press correspondent, and I were covering LBJ in Texas and were invited to his ranch after church services. During our visit, Johnson complained that the cabinet officials, who should have had their resignations on his desk, were dragging their feet. We got the message. Johnson wanted us to write stories that he was waiting for their resignations. He also asked us to use a Washington dateline, even though we were in Texas, to disguise our source. We both did his bidding, although our offices—I worked for UPI then—did not approve of falsifying the dateline. As our exclusive stories moved on the Teletype wires, LBJ phoned Secretary of State Dean Rusk and Defense Secretary Robert S. McNamara and perhaps a few others to tell them to ignore the wire stories, that they did not apply to them.

Other cabinet officials knew the word came from on high and turned in their resignations. No president likes to fire anyone, not even LBJ.

Reporters knew that Johnson could not stand being scooped. If an aide leaked word that Johnson was about to make a top-level appointment and the fact was published, he would postpone or even cancel the appointment.

During the Ronald Reagan presidency, there were two factions: one headed by Chief of Staff James Baker and the other by counselor Edwin Meese, a fellow conservative Californian who had made the long march with Reagan to Washington. The political conflict between the two sides resulted in great leaks to reporters since both men were trying to dominate the news and to prevail with the boss.

A competitive reporter or editor frequently cultivates potential news sources with the hope of receiving information or a tip that will lead to an exclusive story. Sometimes the hot tip is a trial balloon from someone in government. Public officials often talk to a reporter confidentially to get their position out to the public and observe the response. Reporters who give a promise of anonymity are bound to keep their word. It's a matter of trust.

As I mentioned earlier, the most famous "anonymous source" in recent political history was W. Mark Felt, the "Deep Throat" of the Watergate scandal. The *Washington Post* reporting team of Bob Woodward and Carl Bernstein talked to countless secretaries, campaign workers, and aides to government officials. Woodward would meet with Felt, who would either confirm their findings or tell them they were on the wrong track, playing a vital role in steering the story.

In mid-2005, Felt's family decided it was finally time to reveal the role of the ninety-one-year-old man in uncovering the scandal. Woodward said that he, Bernstein, the late *Post* publisher Katharine Graham, and retired executive editor Ben Bradlee had kept the identity of Deep Throat confidential for more than a quarter of a century "because we always keep our promises" to protect an anonymous source.

Newspapers that rely heavily on unnamed sources for stories have learned that it "is a habit that is really hard to break," said Kelly McBride, head of the ethics faculty at the Poynter Institute in St. Petersburg, Florida, a school for professional journalists.

Speaking to James Rainey, a writer for the *Los Angeles Times,* she noted that publications that have strict rules about sources have to be prepared to be scooped occasionally by media who are less restrictive about information, and from whom they get it.

How can journalists best protect their anonymous sources without putting themselves at risk?

The disclosure that former FBI Agent W. Mark Felt was the legendary Deep Throat of Watergate fame, along with the controversies surrounding the reporters involved in the outing of CIA Agent Valerie Plame, has, once again, brought to the forefront the issue of the journalist's privilege.

Throughout American history, it has been the rule rather than the exception that some ideas have clashed with others for acceptance and supremacy. And, Americans have always believed that from the melting pot of ideas, refined by public debate, would flow a better, purer ideal. Many of these clashes have historically taken the form of a battle between constitutional principles. One of those notable, recent illustrations is the doctrine of executive privilege coming into conflict with the powers of Congress. Executive privilege exempts members of the executive branch from disclosing information affecting national security. Presidents have also tried to use it to protect advice they secure. When President Nixon refused to turn over his office tapes to the congressional committee investigating the Watergate break-in, he claimed executive privilege allowed him to withhold the information—a claim the U.S. Supreme Court overruled. Executive privilege was used as a cloak in the Nixon era to attempt to hide his multitude of misdeeds. He wanted no limit to his presidential power.

Watergate, however, represented far more than just a theoretical clash of powers between the executive and legislative branches of government. Equally important, the circumstances of the case, its front-page media exposure, and the methods by which it was uncovered reinforced the American people's belief in the freedoms granted to the press by the First Amendment to the Constitution. Most particularly, this series of events drove home the need for the press to obtain confidential information.

During the Watergate controversy, the free-press questions that arose were peripheral issues. Today, however, these First Amendment freedoms have come to the forefront in a clash with the rights guaranteed to every individual by the Fourth, Sixth, and Fourteenth Amendments to the U.S. Constitution. Moreover, American reporters have long claimed a journalist's privilege—the right of journalists to keep confidential their sources, along with confidential information obtained in newsgathering—including in judicial, legislative, and administrative proceedings. This occasionally conflicts with a prosecutor's desire to get that same information in order to present a persuasive case.

For anyone, going to prison is a daunting experience, but for a reporter or editor simply trying to inform the public, to be jailed or even put under house arrest is a terrifying, humiliating, and depressing experience. We in the media are no braver than anyone else, but journalists know that once they give their word to a source, they have an obligation to keep it. It's that principle that guides them.

The history of the reporter's privilege dates back at least 150 years, and limited support for its foundation can be identified in early developments. During the latter half of the nineteenth century, reporters consistently sought recognition of a privilege in common law. However, this privilege was never recognized by judges, because the basic rule regarding testimony required that anyone properly before the court must testify. The most famous and oft-quoted statement of the principle to the legal bar was (by Professor Wigmore, one of the greatest authorities on the law of evidence) "For more than three centuries, it has now been recognized as a fundamental maxim the public . . . has a right to every man's evidence. When we come to examine the various claims of exemption, we start with the primary assumption that there is a general duty to give what testimony one is capable of giving."

The Fifth Amendment has also experienced some use by reporters to protect their sources. When called upon to testify about a crime that a reporter has seen, the reporter can claim the privilege against self-incrimination—alleging that there could be liability in failing to report a crime to the authorities. Most courts have, however, held that there is no real criminal liability for the reporter, and, therefore, no claim of Fifth Amendment protection. Even if this was permitted, it is obvious that the use of this claim is extremely limited since it can only apply when a crime is witnessed by a reporter.

In the 1950s, Senator Joseph McCarthy, a Wisconsin Republican, went after alleged Communists and "pinkos." Hollywood stars were being hauled up on the witness stand before the House Un-American Activities Committee (HUAC), later abolished by Congress. It was a scary time and led to job losses for many celebrities and the blacklisting of playwrights and actors for their views and associations. As a result, many witnesses "took the Fifth," which to the media of the time implied some guilt. Notable personalities such as the famous actor/producer Charlie Chaplin, a British citizen, fled the United States for more than two decades rather than cooperate with the HUAC investigations. And the late playwright Arthur Miller also refused to cooperate with the committee, which harmed his career for some years. In late 1954, McCarthy was finally stopped when the Senate censured him, 67–22, for abuse of that body during hearings and debates.

Since neither the common law nor the Constitution provide specific federal protection for the nondisclosure of a reporter's sources, many states have attempted to fill the gap, enacting "shield laws." Other states have by court decree recognized either a common-law or a qualified privilege.

Finally, in 1958, the idea of a First Amendment foundation for a reporter's privilege was introduced in the landmark case of *Garland v. Torre,* involving a secret source who said the movie star Judy Garland was overweight. Marie Torre, a syndicated columnist for the former *New York Herald Tribune,* wrote the story. Ironically, from such mundane facts developed a great constitutional debate. Years later, the development of this privilege gathers most of its impetus from the First Amendment, though the degree of protection that journalists enjoy has not been clearly defined. Torre, who stood by her principles, refused a court demand that she reveal her source and spent ten days in prison. Her paper supported her.

Despite the origins of the journalist's privilege in the *Garland* case as a civil issue, the issue began to make headlines in the criminal area, and the contemporary law based upon the First Amendment really developed from these cases. The cases fall into two categories. One area deals with the subpoena of a reporter's notes and a reporter's involvement in testifying before a grand jury. The other area involves the search and seizure of confidential and nonconfidential information by means of a search warrant directed at the news organization or the reporter's files. Given the long history of conflict regarding search and seizures that developed from the British crown's use of general writs to search the homes and offices of colonialists, this is an expected setting for a constitutional privilege to be invoked.

The plurality opinion in the Supreme Court decision in *Branzburg v. Hayes* rejected the existence of a special privilege for reporters and even went so far as to reject the need to prove any special or unusual circumstances before ordering a reporter to testify before a grand jury: "If there is no First Amendment privilege to refuse to answer the relevant and material questions asked during a good-faith grand jury investigation, then it is a fortiori true that there is no privilege to refuse to appear before such a grand jury until the Government demonstrates some 'compelling need' for a newsman's testimony."

Given the court's 1972 opinion in *Branzburg,* it is amazing that the case is cited for the concept that a qualified privilege for reporters does exist. This interpretation resulted from an analysis of Justice Lewis F. Powell's concurring opinion. The plurality opinion by Justice Byron White was joined in by only three other justices. This meant that the concurring opinion of Justice Powell was needed to obtain the fifth vote. Subsequent courts, both state and federal, have relied on Justice Powell's concurrence as, in effect, forming a new majority—and limiting the scope of White's opinion so that, as now interpreted, the decision holds in accordance with Justice Powell: "The asserted claim to privilege should be judged on its facts by the striking of a proper balance between freedom of the press and the obligation of all citizens to give relevant testimony with respect to criminal conduct."

In addition, Justice Powell's ideas were more particularly developed by Justice Potter Stewart's dissent in *Branzburg,* which, in turn, relied upon the lower court's opinion in another case, *Caldwell.* Three basic criteria must be met whenever the government or a criminal defendant wants a reporter to be compelled to testify:

1. There is probable cause to believe the material or relevant information is in a reporter's possession;
2. There is no reasonable alternative means of securing that information; and
3. There is a compelling need for the information and failure to obtain it would result in a miscarriage of justice.

Given this application of rules that, in reality, form a qualified privilege (adopted in different forms by different courts) to criminal cases, it is an easy jump to apply them to civil cases.

Thus, as actually applied, the *Branzburg* case seems to accomplish some of what the press needs. While not absolute, at least a partial privilege has been acknowledged. However, as will be seen, journalists still have a vast area of exposure to far-ranging disclosure requirements.

One of the leading cases on search and seizure involving the journalist's privilege is *Zurcher v. Stanford Daily*. This case arose when, in suppressing a student disturbance at the Stanford University Hospital, nine policemen were injured. No police photographers were at the scene of the assault, nor were there any bystanders to act as witnesses to testify against the assailants. The officers who were injured were only able to identify two of their assailants, but one of them saw at least one individual photographing the altercation. Several days later, a student publication, the *Stanford Daily,* published photographs of the incident, and the paper indicated in its story that one of its reporters had observed the fracas.

The following day a district judge, based on a sworn affidavit, authorized a search warrant. The warrant was issued on a finding of "just, probable, and reasonable cause for believing" that photos and other evidence would be found at the newspaper's office. The police searched the office and seized photographs and notes.

The newspaper filed suit in federal court to bar the use of the search warrant based on a deprivation of rights secured to them by the First Amendment, and to a certain degree by the Fourth and Fourteenth Amendments. The district court and the Court of Appeals agreed with the newspaper, but the Supreme Court did not. The Supreme Court held that a newspaper is no different from any other person and is subject to a search warrant. However, in writing for the majority, Justice White did say that when First Amendment issues are involved, the Fourth Amendment must be applied with "scrupulous exactitude." The Court made no mention of any requirement to give a newspaper any special protection, though the warrant itself should define with "specificity" the place being searched and those items to be seized. The Court also said that in issuing a search warrant, especially one involving First Amendment rights, an overall test of "reasonableness" should be applied. Exactly what this means in practice is open to interpretation.

It is well to remember that in a direct clash with the freedom of the press under the First Amendment in such cases, not only is a news organization being searched, but it is an entity that is not even suspected of any wrongdoing. The seriousness of the infringement upon press rights is clear. There can be physical disruptions to the media organization, as well as the possibility of confidential sources no longer talking to journalists. Reporters for the *Stanford Daily* testified that officers performing the search saw reporters' notes about confidential material in unrelated issues.

Many courts have seen the subpoena as a less offensive intrusion upon the rights of a free press. However, a New Jersey murder trial demonstrates this misguided notion. During the case of *In re Farber,* the defendant issued subpoenas to a *New York Times* reporter, Myron Farber, demanding information that had been given to Farber confidentially. These materials included notes and recordings of his interviews with approximately two hundred people. The New Jersey district court ultimately ordered the production of these materials in camera (in the judge's chambers, in private). When both the *New York Times* and Farber refused, the judge found them both in civil and criminal contempt of court. This decision was, essentially, upheld by the New Jersey Supreme Court, and the U.S. Supreme Court refused to hear it. Because the defendant was ultimately acquitted, without the evidence, no final resolution of this case was achieved. News organizations took up Farber's cause and it was highly publicized.

It is important to note that New Jersey had a shield law that was purported to protect confidential news sources. Yet, despite this law, the Farber court held that the defendant's right to compel witnesses on his behalf, as protected by the Sixth Amendment, was superior to the shield law. In its issuance of the subpoena, the New Jersey Supreme Court did, however, recognize the potential abuse that could impact the First Amendment rights of the press—which is why they directed that the information be delivered to the court in camera.

Nonetheless, even with such precautions, a source may well be deterred, and the free flow of information inhibited simply by knowing that a judge may review the confidential materials. When the source realizes that the judge might allow these materials to be placed in the public record, his or her concern will be magnified. Besides limiting the flow of information, there is also the fear that the government might utilize reporters as investigators for the government. At the very least, there should be a showing on the part of the government that there is no other way to obtain the reporter's materials or information.

The type of "balancing test" that the courts have established with regard to the journalist's privilege has not served reporters well. For instance, they have almost eliminated the privilege when the reporter or media organization is a party to the action, either as a plaintiff or a defendant. Thus, even a qualified privilege is not a sure thing. And, state courts have been quick to place other rights above the First Amendment—even when a shield law exists.

The rights of free speech and free press as created in the First Amendment are the keystone of all of our rights, in my opinion. Therefore, it is difficult to understand why the courts still have such a difficult time developing an organized approach to protecting so important a freedom.

The "outing" of CIA Agent Valerie Plame is a case in point. During the summer of 2003, someone decided to reveal to reporters that former ambassador Joseph Wilson's wife was an undercover CIA agent. Wilson had been a vocal critic of the Bush administration's reasons for waging war on Iraq, discrediting the administration's assertion that Iraq had bought yellowcake uranium from Africa. While several reporters were approached with the information about Valerie Plame, syndicated columnist Robert Novak chose to disclose it, claiming his sources were two anonymous "senior administration officials."

By doing so, Novak might have put both Plame and her foreign sources in jeopardy, and he clearly ended her ability to work as an undercover agent for the CIA. In addition, it is a felony for government officials knowingly to divulge the name of an undercover agent—so Novak may have assisted in a federal crime. Under pressure, the Bush administration subsequently named an independent prosecutor, Patrick Fitzgerald, to get to the bottom of the "leak."

As of this writing, nobody seems to know Novak's status in this investigation. Independent Prosecutor Fitzgerald may have subpoenaed Novak, but no one is certain since grand jury investigations are secret. It is also possible that a gag order was issued, preventing Novak from discussing his testimony if he did appear before the grand jury. Or, maybe Novak never appeared before the grand jury.

It was first assumed that Novak was the first recipient of the leak that Plame was a CIA operative. But it turned out that Bob Woodward of the *Washington Post* was told about Plame in 2003, earlier than Novak. Woodward was working on a book and claimed he did not know the information was classified. But he took a lot of flak for failing to inform the *Post* editors of his role in the controversy.

However, the real problems with the Plame outing are inexplicably related to journalists other than Bob Novak—the author of the original news story. Two reporters, Judith Miller of the *New York Times* and Matthew Cooper of *Time* magazine, were ordered by an appeals court to explain to the grand jury how they learned of Valerie Plame's CIA role. If they refused to reveal their sources, both Miller and Cooper could have faced jail time (and Miller ultimately, of course, was jailed), and their employers could have faced thousands of dollars in fines. Yet, Cooper only reported on the story *after* Novak's column appeared, and Miller, although she made inquiries about the matter, never wrote about it at all.

Despite this, U.S. District Judge Thomas F. Hogan ordered that Judith Miller be jailed until she agreed to tell the grand jury whom she spoke to about the Plame story, citing court decisions that reporters do not have total First Amendment protection from revealing sources. Prior to Miller's confinement, while awaiting a decision from the U.S. Supreme Court, the publisher of the *New York Times*, Arthur Sulzberger Jr., said he was concerned about what this means to journalism: "The pending imprisonment of Judy Miller is an attack on the ability of all journalists to report on the actions of the governments, corporations, and others. The *Times* will continue to fight for the ability of journalists to provide the people of this nation with the essential information they need to evaluate issues affecting our country and the world." Judy Miller ultimately spent eighty-five days in jail on contempt charges. She was released when her source, I. Lewis "Scooter" Libby, gave her a complete waiver to testify before the grand jury. As of this writing, Mr. Libby has been charged with obstruction of justice, false statements, and perjury for allegedly lying about when and how he disclosed classified information to reporters about Valerie Plame.

Matthew Cooper wrote a story saying that the Bush administration had "declared war" on Valerie Plame's husband, former ambassador Joseph C. Wilson, after Wilson had openly criticized the Bush White House. Although not the author of the original piece outing Valerie Plame, Cooper was subpoenaed to appear before Special Prosecutor Fitzgerald's grand jury.

After a motion based on First Amendment grounds to quash Cooper's subpoena was rejected by the U.S. district court in Washington, D.C., he agreed to testify to limited questions about conversations he had with a vice presidential aide. However, Cooper was then subpoenaed a second time. When he refused to reveal his sources, he was held in contempt of court and ordered to jail until agreeing to testify. The sentence was stayed pending appeal.

A three-judge panel of the U.S. Court of Appeals for the District of Columbia, on February 15, 2005, held that no journalist's privilege exists to protect reporters from revealing their confidential sources. The court cited the *Branzburg* case, saying that they did not see any difference in this case.

Matthew Cooper asked the U.S. Supreme Court to review the lower court's decision. His petition for certiorari suggested that during the many decades since *Branzburg* was decided, there have been "significant changes in the legal landscape that strongly support recognition of a federal reporter's privilege." For instance, Congress passed Federal Rule of Evidence 501 in 1975, which says that federal courts should acknowledge new privileges in light of "reason and experience." In the case of *Jaffee v. Redmond* (1996), a new common-law privilege was found for psychotherapists, saying that they are protected from having to testify about their clients. Cooper's petition to the Supreme Court suggested that a reporter's privilege also exists under Federal Rule of Evidence 501—or the First Amendment. Meanwhile, thirty-four states joined forces under an amicus (friend-of-the-court) brief to urge the high court to recognize a reporter's right to keep sources confidential. The movement was led by Utah Attorney General Mark Shurtleff, a Republican.

Other reporters also found themselves caught up in the Valerie Plame affair. Special Prosecutor Fitzgerald subpoenaed Tim Russert of NBC's *Meet the Press,* and Walter Pincus and Glenn Kessler, both of the *Washington Post.* Russert agreed to answer limited questions before the grand jury about his conversations with a vice-presidential aide, so he was not held in contempt. Kessler gave limited testimony by deposition to corroborate that Plame and her husband were not discussed in conversations with a vice-presidential aide. The aide had asked Kessler to affirm this, but did not give Kessler a waiver to reveal the actual content of his conversations. Kessler abided by this. Walter Pincus gave a deposition with an anonymous source's consent, but would not name the source.

In addition, two members of Congress asked Prosecutor Fitzgerald to subpoena James Guckert, who had been writing under the alias Jeff Gannon. Representatives Louise Slaughter (D-N.Y.) and John Conyers (D-Mich.) thought Guckert/Gannon might have been shown a White House memo outing Valerie Plame.

It is important to note that *Branzburg v. Hayes,* the controlling case law after all these years, specifically recognized that Congress would have the right to legislate a federal journalist's privilege "as narrow or broad as deemed necessary." It also said that state legislatures could create state shield laws within their constitutions "so as to recognize a newsman's privilege, either qualified or absolute." According to the Associated Press, thirty-one states, plus the District of Columbia, now have shield laws protecting a journalist from having to reveal confidential sources or confidential information collected in newsgathering.

Given that the courts and legislatures (state and federal) have recognized a variety of other privileges that could strip an accused defendant or prosecutor of possible evidence, it seems the time would be right to recognize the journalist's privilege. For instance, there is a doctor-patient privilege, an attorney-client privilege, and a spousal privilege—and none of these have been interpreted to violate a defendant's or prosecutor's rights. If these "shield" laws are recognized, why not recognize a federal reporter's shield law? Is it not important to the First Amendment, and the free flow of information in this country? The importance of a federal shield law is especially poignant in the cases of the journalists discussed above who faced jail time in the Valerie Plame issue—since the only possible crime committed was by a government official or officials who leaked the information. No journalist had committed a crime.

Finally, the chilling implications of letting *Branzburg* and other cases stand unchallenged may be recognized by Congress. Both houses have bills pending before them that would give journalists a federally recognized privilege in protecting their confidential sources. The journalism community believes a federal shield law is the best answer to prevent further legal action against reporters. According to the Reporters Committee for Freedom of the Press, in 2004 alone, twenty-two reporters received federal subpoenas. This compares to fewer than nine each year from 1991 to 2001. Something needs to be done, and Congress may hold the key.

The federal shield law bill pending in the House of Representatives is cosponsored by Representative Mike Pence (R-Ind.) and Representative Rick Boucher (D-Va.). The Senate's bill was introduced by Senator Richard Lugar (R-Ind.). Senator Chris Dodd (D-Conn.) introduced a similar bill last year, but no action was taken on it. The Reporters Committee for Freedom of the Press has called for a "coordinated effort" to support the bipartisan bills, and former Republican Senate leader Bob Dole wrote a *New York Times* op-ed piece (8/16/05) urging the passage of such a law.

Reporters Committee Executive Director Lucy Dalglish said that these are "perilous times for journalists and the public's right to know. There are more than two dozen cases pending across the United States where journalists are being asked to operate as investigators for the government and litigants. The ability of the media to act as independent sources of information for the public is in jeopardy."

Some ardent supporters of the shield law legislation are concerned that President Bush might not sign it given his hostile attitude toward much of the press. In fact, the Bush Department of Justice is on record opposing the legislation. Deputy Attorney General James B. Comey said the bills were "bad public policy" potentially restricting the administration's efforts to "effectively enforce the law and fight terrorism." This is despite attempts by the legislators to reach a compromise, offering an exception to the shield law in cases where there is an imminent threat to national security.

However, that the bills have support from both sides of the aisle in Congress is a good sign. In an article for *USA Today,* coauthored by Democratic Senator Chris Dodd and Republican Senator Richard Lugar, they write, "An independent press that is free to question, challenge, and investigate is in our nation's best interest—regardless of which political party holds power.

An effective federal shield law would not simply protect the rights of reporters, but all the liberties we cherish as a nation."

Meantime, the U.S. Supreme Court denied certiorari in the reporters' petitions, refusing to hear the Cooper and Miller cases. This meant that the case was kicked back to the lower court, and Judge Hogan immediately ordered the pair to jail. Ultimately, *Time* magazine caved—over the objections of Matt Cooper, turning over his notes—and Cooper then decided to cooperate with the special prosecutor after he was given a waiver of confidentiality from his source, White House operative Karl Rove. Judith Miller was sent to prison.

The Miller case is not without consequences. Immediately following Judith Miller's imprisonment, Cleveland's *Plain Dealer* made it known that it was sitting on "two stories of profound importance." But, because the stories were based on leaked information, the editor of the *Plain Dealer,* Doug Clifton, noted that publishing the stories "would almost certainly lead to a leak investigation and the ultimate choice: talk or go to jail." In addition, Norman Pearlstine, the editor in chief for *Time* magazine, said that *Time* reporters received e-mails from sources after Matt Cooper's notes were turned over to Special Prosecutor Fitzgerald—saying the sources didn't trust the magazine anymore. The chilling implications across the country in media organizations everywhere are evident.

In the future, with or without a federal shield law, the courts must be more careful in attempting to restrict the damage to press rights. The mere assertion that no privilege exists or the setting of limits on the privilege does not relieve the courts of their duty to continue to balance conflicting interests. Newspapers and reporters hold a vital and cherished position in our country. They serve as a counterbalancing factor to excesses that occur in other elements of society—which probably no other institution would expose.

The Watergate outcome was only one of the most recent illustrations of the good that can be accomplished by a free press.

Yet, if Woodward and Bernstein had not been allowed to keep Mark Felt's identity as Deep Throat secret, they may not have been given the information needed to unravel the criminal wrongdoing in the Nixon White House. One cannot imagine these reporters being threatened with jail time like the journalists of today.

Oftentimes, an independent reporter is the only one that has both access and the pulpit needed to effectuate the public good. Repeatedly, throughout history, confidential sources have come forward to journalists who have gotten to the bottom of abuses of power and criminal activity. Many times a reporter is the only individual a potential whistle-blower can rely on. From child abuse issues to safety issues to government abuse of power and corruption to war crimes and political wrongdoing—and everything in between—the press has been the beacon of truth and revelation for the public. If potential sources with information do not believe journalists will keep their confidence, they will probably not come forward to expose the information they possess.

Even the executive branch of the government has understood the need for dispassionate information without public disclosure. This concept was recently reaffirmed in the litigation over Vice President Cheney's energy-policy task force. The Court of Appeals for the District of Columbia held that two groups who sued Cheney did not establish that the government had a legal duty to produce documents regarding White House contact with business leaders and lobbyists. In other words, Cheney argued, and the court agreed, that the confidentiality of internal deliberations between the president and his advisers is constitutionally protected—and necessary for informed decision-making. Because the public does not have the tools of the executive branch of government, it is even more important that they know that they can trust journalists. If a shield law is appropriate for the government, it is certainly appropriate for the press and the public.

I personally thought that since Cheney was doing the public's business, it behooved us to know who was advising him on the nation's crucial oil policy. Going to the court to keep secret who was helping make policy that affected every American opened the door to a suspicion that he only conferred with oil and gas corporation officials.

A reporter's right to protect his or her sources is central to the concept of freedom of the press, and freedom of the press is central to a democracy. This country's early leaders understood the importance of the press. As Abraham Lincoln once said, "Let the people know the facts, and the country will be safe." And Thomas Jefferson said, "Were it left to me to decide whether we should have a government without newspapers, or newspapers without government, I should not hesitate a moment to prefer the latter."

Recognition of the reporter's privilege is the right step in furthering the democratic ideals upon which our country was founded—especially the people's right to know.

CHAPTER 7

NEWSPAPERS ARE A BUSINESS, TOO

The ethical problems of the media and their prickly relationships with secretive government officials are real. But there is a pragmatic side—whether in print or broadcast—and that is how to stay in business in view of rising costs, and dwindling circulations and viewers.

The hand-wringing and genuine concern over the future of newspapers and mainstream media (labeled MSM) goes on with no satisfactory solution in sight.

As competition and costs mount in bringing the news to a public who may feel "overinformed" anyway, publishers and TV executives are trying to stay in business by slashing staff, curbing coverage of events in the United States and abroad, and begging for advertising and readership wherever they can find it. The pressures have been especially hard on the larger publications, such as the *New York Times* and the *Los Angeles Times,* where circulation continues to decline despite the best efforts of the remaining employees on the payroll.

Newspaper circulation has in general been dropping since the 1980s, but the previously discussed scandals on the editorial side of many newspapers, network and cable television channels, and even a few magazines have negatively impacted readership and viewership overall. And with declining advertising, readers, and viewers, the media are in a bind. They don't make widgets; as a service industry, they inform the public.

Financier Warren Buffett, whose company owns an 18 percent interest in the Washington Post Company, recently predicted that the economic health of newspapers will seriously deteriorate in the next two decades—and it's happening already.

Technology has transformed communications and made radio, television, and the Internet preeminent over print in conveying news to the public. Cell phone headlines, digital news, satellite communications, and the basic Internet newspaper Web sites have made an impact on the way news is gathered and delivered to the consumer.

For the six-month period ending March 31, 2005, the Audit Bureau of Circulations (ABC), which oversees advertising rates, reported that daily newspaper circulation nationally fell 1.9 percent, almost double the previous daily decline of about 1 percent on weekdays. Sunday circulation fell 2.5 percent. As the year progressed, help-wanted and online advertising revenue strengthened, although major corporations, such as the auto industry, added relatively little to the bottom line.

The ABC, a membership organization, is relied on by advertisers to monitor newspaper sales, which determines the rates charged for ads, often in the millions of dollars. In an embarrassing scandal related to newspaper advertising, the ABC discovered an overstatement of circulation figures in 2005 involving *Newsday,* on Long Island, New York, owned by the Tribune Company; Belo Corporation's *Dallas Morning News;* and Hollinger International Inc.'s *Chicago Sun-Times.* Federal officials from the U.S. Postal Inspection Service, the Internal Revenue Service, the Securities & Exchange Commission, and other agencies investigated charges of fraud.

Three circulation executives at *Newsday* and its sister publication, the Spanish-language daily *Hoy,* were arrested and could face up to twenty years in prison if convicted of using fake customers, shell companies, and other tactics to overstate the papers' circulation and thus boost the rate charged to advertisers. Their motives were unclear, but the U.S. Attorney's Office for the Eastern District of New York said the scheme "cheated advertisers out of millions of dollars paid for ads in newspapers that were dumped or never paid for." The investigation led to a tightening of the way newspapers determine their circulation count.

The Newspaper Association of America says that media print advertising has been substantially hurt in the past five years by the economic downturn. It would seem that hard times would encourage businesses to get the word out about their products and services, but it is difficult to quantify public relations and advertising success when a company is struggling to make a payroll. The argument can be made that a firm can have the best product or service in the world, but if no one knows about it, what good is it? That is the secret of good advertising.

The association also noted that the National Do Not Call Registry, which went into effect in late 2003, cut heavily into telemarketing sales by publications. Telemarketing used to account for 65 percent of new subscription sales, but the figure dropped substantially as large segments of the public blocked in-home sales calls. The alternative for publications was to use expensive direct mail, television, and radio campaigns—which, of course, benefited the broadcast media.

Veteran media analyst John Morton, describing the newspaper readership crunch, says, "The fact is that newspaper subscribers are dying off at a rate faster than they are being replaced." Television demographers want to appeal to the eighteen-to-forty-nine age group, but newspaper, magazine, and book publishers aren't that choosy. They need readers and subscribers—even if you wrap the fish in an old newspaper the next day.

Morton added, "An economic downturn didn't used to affect circulation all that much. A newspaper was considered almost a utility that people relied on for help-wanted ads and to tell them where you could buy cheap, as well as the news. It's not as true as it used to be" because of Internet access and also free local-community "throwaways," which rely strictly on advertising revenue.

There are also alternative publications and small-town papers away from large metropolitan areas that get the readers' attention and keep them abreast of hometown activities, but it is sad when the world has become a "global village" to see the shrinking of the written word, and reduced foreign news.

To encourage readership, a few smaller papers around the country with Web sites are inviting their readers to contribute to the newspaper by offering their own versions of articles they do not like or by contributing blogs, photos, audio, video, and podcasts in participatory journalism. The *Los Angeles Times* briefly opened its editorial page so readers could go online and add their thoughts to editorials. The experiment was abandoned after only two days when obscene pictures started appearing online from anonymous contributors.

It's not all gloom for the print media, however. Tom Rosenstiel of the Project for Excellence in Journalism says one of the biggest growth areas in the United States and abroad is "ethnic media." Speaking on National Public Radio in 2004, Rosenstiel said his studies show that Spanish-language newspaper circulation has quadrupled to 1.7 million since 1990 compared to an 11 percent overall circulation drop in English-language newspapers in the same period. Spanish-language radio and television has also increased listeners/viewers along with the alternative media, which is targeted to entertainment, lifestyle, sports news, and advertising.

"Spanish-language press obviously has got a cultural orientation that's both covering events overseas that may not be covered in the English press and also covering cultural events in town that may not be covered in the local English-language press," Rosenstiel said. Latinos are the fastest-growing population in the United States.

The Center for American Progress, a liberal think tank, found that nearly two-thirds of Hispanics rely more on Spanish-speaking media for political news than on mainstream English-language media. Ethnic media reach 51 million adults in the United States, with Hispanics the primary consumers. However, the ratio is reversed with other ethnic groups. The poll found that between 60 and 66 percent of African-Americans, Asian Americans, Native Americans, and Arab Americans prefer the mainstream media for political news.

Not surprisingly, advertisers are finding star-focused "gossip" magazines to be a gold mine for marketing to women, who make up the bulk of the celebrity-magazine readership. Most ads in these magazines traditionally offered beauty products and household items, but as working women have become more affluent, marketers are offering ads for cars, pharmaceuticals, and consumer electronics in publications such as *Us Weekly, Star* magazine, *In Touch Weekly,* and others.

Andres Martinez, writing on the op-ed page of the *Los Angeles Times* (4/27/05), commented after the annual American Society of Newspaper Editors (ASNE) meeting in 2005, "Newspapers are undoubtedly in for a period of wrenching change, especially in terms of how the product will be delivered. But we are hardly the equivalent of horse-drawn-buggy manufacturers at the dawn of the automobile era. That's because our core product—thoroughly reported, reliable information—has never been more valuable."

The point-and-click world still depends on old-fashioned reporting and editing for indispensable content, Martinez observed. In other words, the human factor is alive and well in journalism and will remain so.

Mega-publisher Rupert Murdoch of News Corp. Inc., speaking at ASNE, likened the digital hubs Google and Yahoo! to "digital natives" with the rest of the media likened to "digital immigrants." For all of their market value and innovation, Google,

Yahoo!, and the other Internet providers still need wire-service and newspaper input to provide their information services.

"Like Murdoch, I remain optimistic that there is a great deal of opportunity in this migration (of digital immigrants), even if newspaper types in the long run lose control over the distribution of our product," Martinez wrote. "It could happen much as it did when movie studios had to divest their theater chains. Our content, like the studios, will remain valuable on other distribution channels." He envisions an online company eventually buying a media firm to broaden its reach and profitability.

In his informative book *Don't Shoot the Messenger,* Bruce W. Sanford, an expert in First Amendment law, notes, "Profit pressures and preoccupations cannot be dismissed. They are a root cause of the public's cynicism toward the media. Balancing 'church' and 'state' has become a knotty assignment in recent years. The traditional tension between the creative and idealistic part of the communications business and the need to turn a profit has deepened during the past two decades with the arrival of heightened profit expectations."

Sanford added that "profit margins, once deemed respectable at 15 percent, have been pushed north of 20 and even 30 percent in order to impress Wall Street analysts, institutional investors, and portfolio managers everywhere. The judgments that corporate managers make toward the real core of their business—the editorial product—either are made with exquisite sensitivity to the journalistic conscience or the product suffers along with morale.

"No one has warned the public more loudly about the deterioration of the product at the hands of financial barbarians than journalist-advocates themselves—principally because they want to see some semblance of balance preserved in their ongoing dynamic with the accountants."

Political columnist Walter Lippmann said that a free press "should consist of many newspapers decentralized in their ownerships and management, and dependent for their support . . . among the communities where they are written, where they are edited, and where they are read."

Lippmann, who rose to prominence in the middle of the last century, didn't live to see media ownership drop to only fifty companies by 1983. Today, the majority of television, radio, and newspaper operations are controlled by a few companies, with diminishing independent voices.

That's why in 2005, the Public Broadcasting Service, National Public Radio, and hundreds of public radio and TV stations were fighting with Congress for their financial and editorial lives because they were in danger of losing 25 percent—or $100 million—in federal funding, but wiser heads in Congress prevailed.

Congress was considering eliminating money for children's educational programming—Big Bird gone?—satellite technology, and digital-signal improvements, all this in the name of reducing alleged "liberal" influence over public broadcasting.

The *New York Times* had earlier revealed that Kenneth Tomlinson, chairman of the Corporation for Public Broadcasting, had secretly hired Fred Mann, a former member of the right-wing National Journalism Center, to monitor PBS broadcasts with a "liberal slant," particularly those of Bill Moyers and NPR interviewer Diane Rehm. Tomlinson said his goal at the broadcasting corporation was to "strengthen public broadcasting by restoring balance and stamping out liberal bias."

In an effort to placate critics that maintained PBS ignored or marginalized conservative viewpoints in news, science, and documentary shows, PBS unveiled new editorial standards and said it would hire an ombudsman to review controversial programs after they air. PBS does not carry commercials, although most of their programs are underwritten by corporations, which receive on-air credit, an oblique form of advertising, and private donations from viewers.

In a two-page ad in the *Washington Post* (6/21/05), veteran journalist Bill Moyers, now retired, wrote, "Those of us who helped launch public broadcasting were not disdainful of commercial television. We ourselves turned to it for news, diversion, and amusement. We knew that it helped to keep the community dynamic through the satisfaction or creation of appetites. We are a capitalist society, after all. The market is a cornucopia of goods and services, and television programs are part of that market. There is always something to sell, and television can sell. But public television was meant to do what the market will not do. From the outset, we believed there should be one channel not only free of commercials but from commercial values; a channel that does not represent an economic exploitation of life; whose purpose is not to please as many consumers as possible, in order to get as much advertising as possible, in order to sell as many products as possible; one channel—at least one—whose success is measured not by the numbers who watch but by the imprint left on those who do." Moyers's remarks were sponsored by Free Press, a nonpartisan citizens' organization working for a democratic and accountable media.

The Bush administration also took control of the greatly respected Voice of America, which once prided itself on high journalistic standards despite being government-run, and tried to transform it into a propaganda arm in the Middle East and elsewhere. In addition, the administration created two American-sponsored broadcast stations to reach the Arabic-speaking audience in the Middle East in competition with the popular Aljazeera.

In other conservative-versus-liberal activity, Air America, a radio network cofounded by comedian and liberal Al Franken, was slowly gaining ground with seventy stations in mid-2005 in Middle America and a few major cities, although financing was a problem. Even radio giant Clear Channel—bowing to criticism that it was one-sided—said it was also presenting a liberal viewpoint on some of its stations to comment on the Bush administration's conservative policies and the war in Iraq.

Rosenstiel's Project for Excellence in Journalism group

reported in 2004 that twenty-two companies control 70 percent of newspaper circulation; in local television, ten companies own the stations that reach 85 percent of the U.S. population; on the Internet, more than half of the twenty most popular news sites are owned by a handful of the twenty biggest media companies. The Project also noted that newspapers have fewer employees than in 1990—a trend that has grown both in the United States and Europe. The number of network correspondents had dropped by a third since the 1980s, and the number of TV foreign bureaus was down by more than half. The number of full-time radio news employees dropped 44 percent between 1994 and 2001, the report said. The staff reductions continued in all media at the middle of this decade because of economic concerns and advanced technology requiring fewer employees.

The consolidation of media ownership has meant less diversification of viewpoints, but the media left on the playing field remain fiercely competitive in order to survive in an era of one-newspaper towns, conservative politics, entertainment being sold as "news," and computer information at your fingertips. Bloggers online have added to the mix with personal viewpoints providing an interesting public forum for millions of people, although they certainly don't pass as journalists, in my opinion. They are advocates and do not meet the standard of being "fair" in their output.

The Associated Press, the nation's largest remaining wire service providing news to subscribing media, reflects the frustrations of media management as it seeks to become more relevant to changing times. In an article in the *New York Times* (6/20/05), the news-gathering cooperative announced that it has restructured its global operations, resulting in the departure of experienced journalists in Europe and the Middle East. The television networks have made similar cutbacks as media abroad have confronted falling viewership. In the end, it's all about money. Domestically, the AP was considering plans to charge for republication of its articles online, which would put added pressure on publishers who feel economically overburdened by other demands to stay in business.

Reuters Media, part of the British-based Reuters Group, decided to offer multimedia coverage of special events on a dedicated portion of its Web site with the hope of building brand loyalty and capturing a share of the growing online advertising market. Best known for providing financial information and technology to investors and business professionals, the firm noted, "There's a lot more out there than what any single publisher or broadcaster can afford to show you. This is an opportunity to show the world what makes Reuters unique." Reuters has been operating for more than 150 years, but has yet to become a household name in America.

Other economic problems have hit the industry in recent years in the trickle-down economy brought on by outside corporate mergers. An example are grocery-store and department-store mergers over the last two decades. When one store buys another and they combine operations, it means that half of the advertising dollar disappears into a single company. For the food section of a newspaper, for instance, the "weekend specials" at the market shrink, or the section is abandoned, which has happened to many midsize publications nationwide.

"The problem is compounded by a loss in the 1980s of department and grocery store retail ads, which had once been the two biggest sources of retail advertising," according to the Project for Excellence. "As these stores died out or consolidated, the discount retailers that sprang up to replace them, like Wal-Mart and Best Buy, bought little or no newspaper advertising. While this has been going on for decades, it is another long-term pressure on the industry. In the long run, newspapers may have to prove themselves as a medium that can build new audience by offering something that rivals online and elsewhere do not. They need to cover aspects of the community, offer a depth of information, and provide a level of synthesis other media do not."

Other "special features" such as book, theater, music, and

movie reviews and reviewers have also been scaled back in many publications, although "the funny papers" or cartoons that emphasize political issues have survived because Americans like to laugh. And, of course, the sports section is widely read.

On the business pages, some newspapers experimented with cutting or removing stock tables, featuring them only on the newspaper's Web site. New Jersey's *Newark Star-Ledger* cut three pages of its tables in 2001, claiming to save $1 million a year.

Editor & Publisher, the industry magazine, says that readers will interact more and more with a newspaper online, because the Web is more cost-effective for stock statistics, classified ads, TV listings, and even sports box scores.

The argument used to be made that computer research was a generational thing that no one over sixty-five would attempt because it was too complicated, but that idea seems to have fallen away as the information age proliferates and the popularity of the computer continues.

"Fears about the future have been common in news organizations," noted editors/academics John Carey and Nancy Hicks Maynard in the book *The Press.* "In the mid-1990s, the industry's fear was that Microsoft would take over news and classified advertising. Bill Gates was the man to beat. But the threat was vacant. Gates, too, discovered what all publishers know: news, information, and advertising are difficult and expensive to procure. His company bowed out."

Consolidation of media businesses will probably continue, Carey and Maynard said. "The results may be messy in the short term, as they are as each new technology takes hold. News may become more homogenized than is safe for a vibrant democracy. The sacred wall between the newsroom and marketing departments may tatter. A bigger gulf may develop between the old and the young in their news habits, with older Americans continuing to read daily newspapers and watch network news, and younger consumers watching cable, surfing the Web, and reading specialty magazines."

Carey and Maynard concluded, "The American public has had a way of finding the right answers, at the right time, for policies that matter most. If we are a somnolent society when it comes to policy, history shows that we sleep with one eye open and pay attention when we must. The core role of journalists and news organizations in providing citizens with an accurate and informed picture of people and events is not likely to change, although there may be some adjustments to be made as new technologies take hold. And while technology and business forces may shape how news is delivered and consumed—not always to the benefit of society—it will still be left to professional and committed journalists to determine the quality of what is created and how it serves the needs of citizens in a democracy."

So, the beat goes on. The media will survive in this democracy, as it always has, but the "times they are a-changin'" and it is necessary to change with them to survive.

CHAPTER 8

THE FCC—FAIR AND BALANCED?

If newspapers are a business, the broadcast media are even more so. Profits—rather than concern for the people's right to know—dominate the industry. The fairness doctrine has been tossed out the window. Entertainment is the name of the game except in a national catastrophe. And the FCC has been rendered powerless by deregulation.

All regulatory acts in the United States have immense social, political, and economic impact. This is especially true when the regulated activity involves the First Amendment and the concept of free speech. Governments around the world have used state control of broadcasting to implement and enforce their specific doctrines. For example, the government-run media of the former Soviet Union used its power to control information perhaps more completely than any other society in history.

At the same time, there clearly are legitimate needs for some government regulation. For instance, an extremely limited number of bandwidths are available in traditional broadcasting, so there must be a fair way to allocate those bandwidths. Inherently, these limits can either narrow or broaden free speech—ultimately to the point where pornography and hate-mongering are freely disbursed or regulations are put into place. Because of the overall pervasiveness of the broadcasting industry, and its ability to reach virtually everyone in the United States, these issues are of paramount importance—not just to business, but also to people's everyday lives.

The Federal Communications Commission, commonly referred to as the FCC, was created by an act of Congress on June 19, 1934. Its purpose is to "make available to all the people of the United States, without discrimination, a rapid, efficient nationwide, and worldwide wire and radio communication service with adequate facilities at reasonable charges." Created during the New Deal era, with President Franklin D. Roosevelt's backing, the commission was given broad powers. Its jurisdiction includes all fifty states and territories, and it reports directly to Congress. The FCC's current power to regulate the communications industry is rooted in the Communications Act of 1934.

Originally, the FCC had 233 employees who worked to coordinate the separate rules and regulations of the Interstate Commerce Commission, the Federal Radio Commission, and the postmaster general—which initially divided the power to regulate the communications industry. The 1934 act stipulated a body made up of seven commissioners, who would be appointed by the president and confirmed by the Senate, to direct the business of the FCC.

Today, the Federal Communications Commission has around nineteen hundred employees, and the scope of its powers to regulate the communications industry was expanded under the Communications Satellite Act of 1962. This act gave the FCC regulatory powers over radio and television broadcasting, telegraph, telephone, two-way radio, satellite communications, and cable television.

In addition, in 1983, the number of FCC commissioners was reduced from seven to five, and they continue to be appointed by the president with Senate confirmation. Only three of the five commissioners can be from the same political party, and none can have a financial stake in any FCC-regulated business. The president chooses one of the five commissioners to act as the chair of the FCC. Each of the commissioners, including the chair, serves a five-year term (except when an unexpired term is filled).

Traditionally, the chair of the FCC resigns when a new president is elected. The chair holds a powerful position in that he or she sets the course of action for the commission and also appoints departmental and bureau heads. Thus, this seemingly nonpartisan body can become politicized depending upon the chair's personality and agenda, whom the White House designates as chair, and his or her ties to the communications industry.

The original 1934 Communications Act has been amended numerous times. Many of these changes are a result of changes in technology that have taken place over time (e.g., the advent of traditional television, cable television, satellite communications, cellular phones, and other communications means). This broadening of powers to regulate the "new" technologies is sometimes shared with other federal agencies now, but the original act is broad enough to allow the commission to retain general control over most communications issues.

The most important powers bestowed upon the FCC include its powers to license, renew licenses, and revoke licenses of broadcast entities. The commission's authority in granting or revoking such licenses is predicated on the notion that the airwaves belong to the public, and therefore broadcasters should take into consideration the "public interest, convenience, and necessity" in deciding what to air. When I covered the FCC in the 1950s, the public interest seemed to be the defining element in granting radio and TV licenses. The applications for broadcast channels were closely scrutinized, and the applicants' backgrounds were carefully screened.

Of course, exactly what embodies the "public interest, convenience, and necessity" is a matter of interpretation, based upon the views of the five commissioners of the FCC. And too often lately, this interpretation seems to favor big-business economic interests over the "public" interest.

However, public-interest regulation has proved to be an area of bustling activity and disagreement for the FCC. These areas encompass a number of broadcasting content issues including obscene or indecent programming, political editorials, children's programming, and certain types of advertising. Whether the Federal Communications Commission has effectively upheld the public interest in its decisions is debatable.

From its inception, the FCC (along with the courts) has claimed that due to the nature of the broadcast medium, not everyone will have access to the airwaves in the same way people have access to other media. While people are free to speak and write in other types of arenas, there are a finite number of broadcast spectrums available, and therefore not everyone can have access to them. Those individuals privileged to use the airwaves implicitly agree that the interests of the viewers and listeners must be predominant, rather than the interests of the broadcasters themselves—but in practice we don't see that happening.

The Supreme Court first recognized this issue in *National Broadcasting Co., Inc. v. United States,* in 1943 during the "radio era." In this case, the Court said that denying a broadcast license or frequency on the grounds of the public interest is not a violation of free speech under the First Amendment. Justice Frankfurter wrote, "Freedom of utterance is abridged to many who wish to use the limited facilities of radio. Unlike other modes of expression, radio inherently is not available to all. That is its unique characteristic and that is why, unlike other modes of expression, it is subject to governmental regulation." In addition, Frankfurter said that the most important interest to be considered has to be "the interest of the listening public."

How far the FCC can go in regulating the broadcasting industry in the public's interest was further delimited in *Red Lion Broadcasting Co. v. Federal Communications Commission* (1969). In this case, a company challenged the FCC's right to mandate that broadcasters adhere to the "fairness doctrine," the first such challenge based on a constitutional rationale of the First Amendment's right of free speech. The fairness doctrine mandated that broadcasters allow a response to personal attacks or political editorials.

In *Red Lion,* the Supreme Court unanimously rejected the idea that there is an identical right to free speech in broadcasting to that which exists in published or spoken speech: "Where there are substantially more individuals who want to broadcast than there are frequencies to allocate, it is idle to posit an unabridgeable First Amendment right to broadcast comparable to the right of every individual to speak, write, or publish." The Court went on to say that under some circumstances the public interest requires a broadcast licensee to allow "those views and voices which are representative of his community and which would otherwise, by necessity, be barred from the airwaves." Therefore, the rights of the broadcast licensees must be ancillary to the rights of viewers and listeners who want exposure to new ideas.

In fact, sections of the Supreme Court's opinion almost seemed to hold that a fairness doctrine is constitutionally mandated: "It is the right of the public to receive suitable access to social, political, esthetic, moral, and other ideas and experiences which is crucial here. That right may not constitutionally be abridged either by Congress or by the [Federal Communications Commission]."

Subsequently, however, the Supreme Court made clear that there is not a carte blanche right of access to the airwaves. In *Columbia Broadcasting System v. Democratic National Committee,* the Court held that the First Amendment does not require the sale of advertising time to groups, even if state action is involved. The CBS decision said that competing interests must be balanced in granting access to broadcasting: "Only when the interests of the public are found to outweigh the private journalistic interests of the broadcasters will government powers be asserted within the framework of the [Federal Communications] Act."

However, in *C.B.S., Inc. v. F.C.C.* (1981), the Court held that a narrowly constructed statute providing limited access was constitutional. A law giving qualified candidates for federal office a right to buy broadcasting time, without consideration as to whether an opponent had bought time, was upheld. Without providing for any "general right of access to the media," the Supreme Court said the law in question balances the rights of all those involved because it "creates a limited right to 'reasonable' access that pertains only to legally qualified federal candidates and may be invoked by them only for the purpose of advancing their candidacies once a campaign has commenced."

Thus, the fairness doctrine was never absolute, and more recent cases have eroded it further, ultimately resulting in its abolition in 1987 during Ronald Reagan's deregulation era. Reagan's antiregulation FCC chair, Mark S. Fowler, rejected the idea that broadcasters have a unique responsibility to insure that a broad range of ideas are presented on controversial issues. He said television is "just another appliance—it's a toaster with pictures." And this viewpoint was crystallized in Fowler's goal to repeal the fairness doctrine, though it was not actually abolished until a few months after he left the FCC. It makes you wonder if in fact the airwaves do really belong to the public.

Mark Fowler and other Reagan appointees to the FCC claimed that the fairness doctrine was an infringement on broadcasters' First Amendment rights and actually had a "chilling" effect on debate. This was true, they argued, because of government intrusions on editorial control, as well as constant fear by broadcasters that their licenses would be revoked if they refused to comply with citizens' demands for response time. And, why not? Why should the broadcasters have that much control over an outlet that belongs to all the American people?

In reality, the FCC refrained from enforcing the fairness doctrine beginning in the mid-1980s—prior to its actual repeal. But, the deregulation commissioners set out to entirely eliminate the 1959 amendment to the Communications Act that had made the doctrine reality. Two Reagan appointees to the U.S. Court of Appeals, who obviously shared the deregulation commissioners' views, assisted Mark Fowler's vision.

In a 2–1 decision, Judges Robert Bork and Antonin Scalia (later appointed to the U.S. Supreme Court) held, "We do not believe that language adopted in 1959 made the Fairness Doctrine a binding statutory obligation," since the doctrine was established "under"—rather than "by"—the 1934 Communications Act. Therefore, the FCC was under no obligation to enforce the fairness doctrine. Its fate was sealed in 1987 during the Reagan administration when the new FCC chair and former Reagan aide Dennis R. Patrick rescinded the doctrine—par for the course. This is just one more way in which deregulation has hurt the ordinary citizen and helped special interests.

There have been bills in Congress to try to restore the fairness doctrine, but none has been successful. One, introduced shortly after the doctrine's repeal, passed Congress, but without enough votes to override President Reagan's veto. Another bill was dead in the water when President George Bush-1 threatened to veto it.

Why, one might ask, is the concept of a fairness doctrine so important to a democratic society? In a study conducted by the Media Access Project (MAP), in conjunction with the Benton Foundation, and reported in the *Federal Communications Law Journal,* it was shown that the repeal of the fairness doctrine has led to one-quarter of all broadcast entities denying the public any local news or public affairs programming. And Robert F. Kennedy Jr. has written, "The FCC's pro-industry, antiregulatory philosophy has effectively ended the right of access to broadcast television by any but the moneyed interests." Or, as Representative Maurice Hinchey (D-N.Y.) said, "In a free and open society, in a democratic republic, you need a free and open discussion of the issues. We don't have that today."

In a recent poll taken by Media Matters for America, it was found that voters monumentally champion the idea of restoring "balance" and "fairness" to broadcasting. Asked if television and radio stations using public airwaves should be compelled to present both sides of an issue, 77 percent of likely voters said they should. In addition, 74 percent of conservatives agreed. What is it that American citizens understand that the FCC and other government officials don't get?

Following the recision of the fairness doctrine, we have discerned a clear, upward swing in partisan "news"—with no ramifications for the broadcasters. Conservative talk show hosts such as Bill O'Reilly and Rush Limbaugh dominate the airwaves, never blinking an eye at their one-sided presentation of the issues. In fact, a 1993 attempt by Congress to reinstate the fairness doctrine resulted in Limbaugh and his supporters rallying against the "Hush Rush Law." This is fallacious on the face of it. Rush Limbaugh and his like certainly have a right to be on the air, but in a democratic society where the exchange of ideas is paramount to an informed public, we have an obligation to insure that exchange occurs, offering more than one point of view. I regret they could be mistaken for journalists.

It is a slippery slope if we continue to allow the presentation of one side of an issue without presenting the other. No democracy can function without a truly informed citizenry—and that includes information from many perspectives. Without a requirement to present different viewpoints, what is to stop a power-hungry individual or the government from seeing to it that theirs is the only philosophy disseminated? The airwaves are limited, and the danger in also limiting access to the airwaves is obvious. Fox boasts in its slogan that it is "fair and balanced," but its audiences know they are consistently bombarded with a pro-administration, conservative viewpoint.

When, just days before the 2004 presidential election, Sinclair Broadcasting, which reaches 25 percent of the country's population, revealed its intention to air an anti-Kerry documentary on all of its affiliates, they were forced to relent in the face of public outrage, a boycott by advertisers, and falling stock prices.

The Sinclair Broadcasting dilemma also demonstrates the dangers inherent in putting the power of the airwaves in a limited number of owners' hands. The conglomeration of media ownership into fewer and fewer hands elevates the importance of the fairness doctrine since the lack of diversity in broadcasting ownership can result in limited viewpoints—and opens the door to conflicts of interest. If media consolidation weren't such a big issue, the impact on the fairness doctrine would be lessened—though its importance would not. At the same time, the "liberal" point of view has virtually been ruled off the air in the current political climate—and the word *liberal* has been demonized.

Diversity of ownership in the broadcasting arena has been another area of discourse for the FCC, and its importance cannot be dismissed. As Representative Maurice Hinchey once said, media consolidation "is the most critical issue facing the American people today: whether to allow a handful of people to determine what information we receive and influence the decisions we make."

It is hard to visualize a situation where a few companies would own all of the media outlets, but its impact would be devastating to the marketplace of ideas and viewpoints. Imagine Fox with its conservative slant controlling the vast majority of market share, or imagine Air America with its liberal slant presiding over most of the media. People would no longer be exposed to opposing perspectives—and, therefore, they would no longer be informed voters. The dangers to democracy are obvious.

Throughout the history of the FCC, various rules have come into play with regard to media ownership. The "Seven Station Rule" restricted the number of stations that could be owned by an individual media corporation, and multiple-ownership/cross-ownership limits have been applied. But, in 1985, the Federal Communications Commission began whittling away at many of the rules in place. With a pro-business inclination, many on the

FCC claimed that the advent of "new" technologies (such as cable television and the Internet) attested to the need for a change in the rules—given that news is no longer fully governed by newspapers and broadcast radio and television.

However, on June 13, 2005, the U.S. Supreme Court refused to hear an appeal of a lower-court decision holding that the FCC had not satisfactorily justified its 2003 relaxation of ownership regulations. The new rules promulgated by the commission would have made it easier for one company to own both a television station with the highest ratings, and a newspaper with the biggest circulation, in the same market. In addition, the rules would have allowed large companies to own more television and radio stations.

But when the new regulations were set to be implemented, the U.S. Court of Appeals for the Third Circuit said that the methods used by the FCC to decide how many stations can be owned by a single company in the same market were inadequate. For now, at least, this decision stands. Nonetheless, because the court did not weigh in on the merits of the ownership rules (only the methodology used), many predict that the FCC will attempt to draft another, similar set of rules reflecting their misguided views on media concentration. The public should be concerned.

The seven largest media companies already control 80 percent of our access to information. If the FCC moves ahead with its deregulation of ownership rules, it is conceivable that only a handful of corporate conglomerates will dominate the entire market. Even Ted Turner, the founder of CNN, has said that the new rules could "stifle debate, inhibit new ideas, and shut out smaller businesses trying to compete."

Congressman Bernie Sanders (I-Vt.) summed up the issue well when he said the FCC rules "will lead to even fewer media giants owning and controlling what people see, hear, and read in America. That's truly dangerous because the health of our democracy depends on multiple viewpoints being debated. When you have only a few companies controlling everything, you get one corporate view." Sanders then said, "This is not a partisan issue or an ideological one. You have people all over the political spectrum fighting against [the FCC rules]—from consumer groups to the Catholic bishops to the NRA—because they know what a danger this new rule is. It will be frightening when we wake up one day and find that three or four huge conglomerates control the flow of information in this country."

At the turn of the twentieth century, we had President Theodore Roosevelt going after the monopolies and cartels. People understood that the public good was being sacrificed at the altar of the plutocracies. But where are the American people today in demanding diverse ownership of the airwaves? And where is Congress when they should be stopping the overreach of the giant broadcasting conglomerates?

CHAPTER 9

LAPDOGS OF THE PRESS

For all the unhappy trends I have witnessed—conservative swings on television networks, dwindling newspaper circulation, the jailing of reporters and "spin"—nothing is more troubling to me than the obsequious press during the run-up to the invasion of Iraq. They lapped up everything the Pentagon and the White House could dish out—no questions asked.

That was the immediate post-9/11 period. They have had a grand awakening.

Reporters and editors like to think of themselves as watchdogs for the public good. So do professional journalism organizations that set ethical guidelines and strict rules for membership. But in recent years, both individual reporters and their ever-growing corporate ownership have defaulted on that role. Ted Stannard, an academic and former UPI correspondent, put it this way: "When watchdogs, bird dogs, and bulldogs morph into lapdogs, lazy dogs, or yellow dogs, the nation is in trouble."

Subdued by the political climate in the country in the aftermath of the 9/11 terrorist attacks, reporters pulled their punches and refrained from asking the tough questions that should have been posed to the president and White House spokesmen on subjects ranging from homeland security to the economy.

They forgot their credo that an eternal spotlight on public officials was the best way to keep them honest. In the long run-up to the Iraq War, reporters were bombarded with misleading information and "spin" from the government, which was played in the press as gospel.

Correspondents who were supposed to stick to the facts in their news stories and some editors who were supposed to play the news straight seemed to take their cues from the bias of the editorial pages of their newspapers during wartime.

As the war went on, and on, the soul-searching on the part of the mainstream media began in earnest. Newspapers became confessional, admitting they had missed the boat and promising to be more scrupulous in the use of anonymous sources. They also began to hire ombudsmen to keep a critical eye on their news output and to keep the pressure on their reporters to refrain from what was called "hit-and-run" journalism in *The Press,* edited by Geneva Overholser and Kathleen Hall Jamieson.

The naive complicity of the press and the government was never more pronounced than in the prelude to the invasions of Afghanistan and Iraq. The media became an echo chamber for White House pronouncements. Sadly, too, many statements were misleading and false on both sides. Reporters became stenographers instead of interrogators.

Critics are still wondering why White House reporters were so quiescent at President Bush's March 6, 2003, news conference, which was scripted and in which he made it eminently clear that the United States was going to war. We invaded Iraq two weeks later.

One reporter present pleased the "born-again" Bush when she asked him if he prayed about going to war. And so it went. White House reporters became a laughingstock before the viewing public, who wondered about all the "softballs" being pitched to the president at such a momentous time. Few reporters doubted that war was inevitable, and even fewer probed his reasons for such a drastic decision.

After all, two of the nation's most prestigious newspapers, the *New York Times* and the *Washington Post,* had kept up a drumbeat for war with Iraq to bring down dictator Saddam Hussein. They accepted almost unquestioningly the bogus evidence of weapons of mass destruction, the dubious White House rationale that proved to be so costly on a human scale, not to mention a drain on the treasury.

Another question is, Why was the administration's lack of credibility so unclear?

President Bush's self-proclaimed desire to be known as a "war president," even before the terrorist attacks on the World Trade Center in New York and the Pentagon on 9/11, should have triggered some skepticism. In fact, in a preelection interview with a *Houston Chronicle* reporter, he had said he wanted to be known as a war president.

The *Washington Post* was much more hawkish than the *Times,* but both newspapers played into the hands of the administration. The *Post* ran many editorials pumping up the need to wage war against the Iraqi dictator.

The trusted secretary of state, Colin Powell, was the stalking horse for the administration, leading the way to Baghdad, when he delivered his seventy-six-minute boffo statement on Hussein's lethal toxic arsenal on February 5, 2003, before the United Nations. Nothing more had to be said. Bush counted on Powell's credibility and public marketability to sell his war, and it worked.

Powell was a good soldier. He struggled to make the facts fit his case for war, paying several visits to CIA headquarters in preparing his UN statement. He served his commander in chief well, while shortchanging the American people, who have the right to know the truth and even share the doubts.

The national press went overboard in praising Powell's speech, according to the *Columbia Journalism Review,* which cited the *Washington Post* as saying his presentation was irrefutable. The *New York Times* said he left "little question that Mr. Hussein had tried hard to conceal" a so-called smoking gun or weapons of mass destruction (WMD).

With the administration steadily staying on message for two years, the country, still traumatized by the terrorist attacks, was easily convinced that Saddam Hussein possessed weapons of mass destruction, had ties to the Al Qaeda terrorist network, and was a threat to the United States.

The British went even further in their buildup for war. Prime Minister Tony Blair's government warned that Saddam was capable of attacking Europe or America in forty-five minutes, a "fact" that was repeated by members of the Bush administration. Two U.S. special weapons-inspection task forces, headed by chief weapons inspector David Kay and later by Charles Duelfer, came up empty in the scouring of Iraq for WMD, after spending months and millions of dollars in the country.

Did you hear any apologies from the Bush administration? Of course not. It simply changed its rationale for the war—several times. The last reason given—and they stuck to it—was that the United States wanted to spread democracy in the Middle East.

Nor did the media say much about the failed weapons search. Several newspapers made it a front-page story, but with only one-day coverage. The *New York Post* apparently did not think it was news, according to former CBS-TV London correspondent Tom Fenton, author of *Bad News.*

As for Colin Powell, he simply lost his halo when no unconventional weapons were found in Iraq. After that, he publicly retreated on the salient points of his UN speech, but the newspapers played his backpedaling inconspicuously on the back pages. The reward for this loyalty was his replacement as secretary of state in Bush's second term by Condoleezza Rice. But Powell did not long remain silent after he left the Bush cabinet. He told Barbara Walters in an ABC-TV interview that his UN performance is a painful "blot" on his career, and that blot will blemish his record for the rest of his life.

No weapons. No ties to terrorists. No threats. No apologies.

No explanations. No remorse. Under those circumstances, Americans were told they were fighting a war in Baghdad for liberty and democracy throughout the Middle East. Bush could shift the rationale in the blink of an eye with no apparent qualms.

And, of course, it was important to support the troops in Iraq. Reporters were left to follow the administration's lead. Anything less would have been seen as "unpatriotic." The nation paid a heavy price for the media's blind trust. The administration, which never lacked for chutzpah, rode out the storm with its credibility in the tank and few reporters daring to push President Bush on his flimsy reasons for invading Iraq.

My concern is why the nation's media were so gullible. Did they really think it was all going to be so easy, a cakewalk, a superpower invading a third world country? Why did the Washington press corps forgo its traditional skepticism? Why did reporters become cheerleaders for a deceptive administration?

Could it be that no one wanted to stand alone outside Washington's pack journalism? Several columnists and editorial writers bought the Bush line that there had to be a regime change in Iraq with Saddam Hussein deposed because the dictator had killed thousands of his own people.

On August 20, 2004, Tribune Media Services editor Robert C. Koehler's column published in the *San Francisco Chronicle* summed it up best: "Our print media pacesetters, the *New York Times,* and just the other day, the *Washington Post,* have searched their souls over the misleading prewar coverage they foisted on the nation last year, and blurted out qualified Reaganesque mea culpas: 'Mistakes were made.' "

Koehler was sure that no one would take the fall: "When the war drum sounds, big media dances. It's as simple as that." He wrote that ultimately the newspapers found themselves "guilty of nothing worse than occasionally questionable judgment in story selection."

The *Washington Post*'s media critic, Howard Kurtz, who claims he decided on his own to write a three-thousand-word retrospective on the *Post*'s coverage of the war, played up heavily the newspaper's defense of hindsight.

"No one in management asked me to write the story," Kurtz wrote. "As the paper's media reporter, I simply felt that there were many lingering questions, both inside and outside the newsroom, that cried out for an in-depth assessment of the *Post*'s prewar reporting on WMDs."

Kurtz said, "The most intense anger toward the mainstream media seems to be coming from the liberal side, especially liberals who passionately opposed the invasion of Iraq and see the nation's top news organizations as essentially having aided and abetted President Bush in his march to war."

Kurtz acknowledged that there "was a consistent pattern of administration declarations about Iraq being trumpeted on the *Post*'s front page month after month while most of the skeptical stories, despite complaints from reporters involved, were assigned to inside pages."

"Overall, in retrospect, we underplayed some of those [skeptical] stories," *Post* Executive Editor Leonard Downie Jr. was quoted as saying.

In his critique, Koehler noted that Downie complained that critics "have the mistaken impression that somehow if the media's coverage had been different, there wouldn't have been a war." Maybe Downie should reread the scores of editorials the *Post* carried before the war urging an attack on Iraq.

He certainly underestimated the power of the press and the elation of the administration to have the backing of the *Post* with its vast official audience and global diplomatic impact. Downie acknowledged that questionable reporting methods plus outright fabrication and plagiarism have undoubtedly shaken public trust in the media.

He said the *Post,* like other news organizations, was reviewing its policies "on accuracy, fairness, and our relationships with news sources and readers." Also under study, Downie said, was the "use of confidential sources and corrections of our mistakes."

Downie noted, "Furthermore, we want to be first with news, but we also want to be right." He promised "to identify whenever possible the sources of the information we publish in our reporting."

On May 26, 2004, the *New York Times* published what it described as a "self-critical" note to its readers apologizing for the paper's "sometimes erroneous reporting on weapons of mass destruction in Iraq" before the March 2003 invasion of Iraq and during the early days of the occupation.

In a mea culpa, yet to be emulated in the *Washington Post,* the *Times* editors said, "Readers, other journalists, and some antiwar politicians have argued that the paper's numerous stories suggesting that Saddam Hussein may have constructed a large weapons of mass destruction program helped bolster the Bush administration's arguments for going to war. No such weapons have been found.

"Over the past year, this newspaper has shone the bright light of hindsight on decisions that led the United States into Iraq," the *Times* continued. "We have studied the allegations of official gullibility and hype. It is past time we turned the same light on ourselves."

The contrite editors said they wished they had been more aggressive in looking at information provided by a "circle of Iraqi informants, defectors, and exiles bent on 'regime change' in Iraq, people whose credibility has come under increasing public debate."

In a special "note," the *Times* told readers that editors at several levels "who should have been challenging reporters and pressing for more skepticism were too intent on rushing scoops into the paper."

Times reporter Judith Miller (later jailed in the Valerie Plame–related investigation) reportedly relied heavily on Iraqi defector Ahmad Chalabi, who was on the Pentagon payroll. Chalabi at one time had been a banker in Jordan, convicted there of embezzling millions of dollars. Miller wrote many front-page stories on the Iraqi possession of unconventional weapons.

After the United States invaded and occupied Iraq, Chalabi acknowledged that some of his claims of Iraqi arsenals were off-base, but he bragged that he had at least achieved his goal to get American troops into the country. Even after that deception, he was made Iraqi oil minister.

When queried about the editorials boosting the war, Gail Collins, who was in charge of the *New York Times* editorial page, told the *Columbia Journalism Review,* "I will go off my normal rule to say I wish we had known there were no weapons of mass destruction."

But Janet Clayton of the *Los Angeles Times* editorial pages said it better: "I do wish we'd been more skeptical of Powell's WMD claims before the United Nations."

Reporters had their opportunities, day after day at the White House and the Pentagon, to cut through the nonsense that the administration was promoting to instigate the war, but most of the correspondents played along, not daring to hold to the fire the feet of Bush's spokesmen Ari Fleischer and Scott McClellan, or on rare occasions, the president himself.

The air of inevitability about the forthcoming war may have played a part in inhibiting reporters, but I thought the administration had a lot of explaining to do.

Not all the blame can be laid at the doorstep of the print media. CNN's war correspondent, Christiane Amanpour, was critical of her own network for not asking enough questions about WMD. She attributed it to the competition for ratings with Fox, which had an inside track to top administration officials.

Tom Fenton also gave a scathing indictment of television's network executives for ignoring the foreign correspondents' warnings of Islamic fundamentalist hostility. Fenton, who spent years as a Middle East correspondent, tried in vain to get his network to support his attempts to interview Osama bin Laden, but CBS was not interested.

It was painful to read in the *Nation* the results of two studies of unsigned newspaper editorials supporting the administration in the run-up to the Iraq invasion. The surveys, one by Michael Massing in the *New York Review of Books* (2/26/05) and the other by Chris Mooney in the March-April 2005 *Columbia Journalism Review,* painted a picture of a timid, credulous press corps that, when confronted by an administration intent on war, "sank to new depths of obsequiousness and docility."

Massing gave high marks to the Knight Ridder Washington Bureau, whose hard-hitting stories were based on "doubts and fears of military, intelligence, and diplomatic officials, many of whom believed that the White House was misinterpreting and fabricating evidence about Iraq's bellicosity."

Despite the apologies of the mainstream press for not having vigilantly questioned before and in the early stages of the war the evidence of WMD and links to terrorists, the newspapers dropped the ball again by ignoring for days a damaging report in the *Times* of London on May 1, 2005, that revealed the so-called Downing Street Memo (minutes) describing a high-powered, confidential meeting that British Prime Minister Tony Blair held with his top advisers on Bush's forthcoming plans to attack Iraq. At the secret session, Richard Dearlove, former head of British intelligence, had just returned from Washington where he'd conferred with national security officials and told Blair that President Bush "wanted to remove Saddam Hussein through military action, justified by the conjunction of terrorism and WMD. But the intelligence and facts were being fixed around the policy."

None of the facts in the minutes were disavowed by the government. When Blair met with the president in early June 2005, both of them tap-danced around the issue, noting that they had put the case against Saddam to the UN Security Council before going to war. The UN pitch was all a charade. Clearly, war was on the agenda for both Bush and Blair for many months. There are strong indications Bush had war with Iraq in mind even before he went into the White House. The $64 question is, Why was he so obsessed with Saddam?

The Downing Street Memo was a bombshell when discussed by the bloggers, but the mainstream print media ignored it until it became too embarrassing to suppress any longer. The *Washington Post* discounted the memo as old news and pointed to reports it had published many months before on the buildup to the war. Besides, foreign editor David Hoffman said the memo was leaked close to the British elections and the paper did not have the manpower to check it out.

The paper did carry the story some ten days later, again on the back pages.

Los Angeles Times editorial page editor Michael Kinsley decided that the classified minutes of the Blair meeting were not a "smoking gun." He felt it was not proof that Bush was determined to invade Iraq a year before he gave the green light. "I don't buy the fuss," Kinsley said.

The *New York Times* touched on the memo in a dispatch during the last days leading up to the British elections, but put it in the tenth paragraph. Philip Taubman, the *Times* Washington Bureau chief, said it did not "seem like a bolt out of the blue" in view of the previous war-plan reporting.

USA Today, questioning the timing of the leak four days before the British elections, did not mention the memo and was unable to get it through its own sources.

National Public Radio's ombudsman, Jeffrey Dvorkin, said it "seemed like confirmation of what is already known in the United States, but it still is an extraordinary memo."

Representative John Conyers (D-Mich.) joined the dustup, obtaining 560,000 signatures on a petition presented at the White House gate demanding that the president explain the memo's allegations that prewar intelligence had been "fixed around" Bush's intention to invade Iraq.

"After the abject failure of the media to expose the myth of WMD and Iraq, the cheerleading coverage of 'embedded' reporters, and the transmission of propaganda to the American people . . . aren't we owed some good sustained and thorough reporting on this?" Conyers wrote on Arianna Huffington's blog.

Meanwhile, a survey of about fifteen hundred Americans by the Pew Research Center for the People and the Press in mid-2005 found overwhelming dissatisfaction with news organizations, with a rising number of people saying that the news media were "too critical of America." Pew said the survey showed an increasing political polarization of the country.

The scrutiny of the role of the limpid press in helping to promote the Iraq War, if only by its silence, took me back to the days immediately following the unraveling of the Watergate scandal. The White House press corps realized it had fallen asleep at the switch, not that all the investigative reporting could have been done by those on the "body watch" of traveling everywhere with the president with no time to dig for facts. But looking back, the press corps knew that they had missed many clues on the Watergate scandal and were determined to become much more skeptical at what was being dished out to them at the daily briefings. And, indeed, they were. The White House pressroom became a lion's den. Nothing was accepted at face value. President Ford's press secretary Ron Nessen and later Jody Powell, President Carter's spokesman, got the brunt of a hostile, newly awakened press for a time.

But the current reporters are a new generation covering the White House, and it's a different administration—and both sides had much to learn following 9/11 and the increase of terrorism around the world.

When the White House lost its credibility in rationalizing the preemptive assault on Iraq, the correspondents began to come out of their coma. And yet, they were still too timid to confront and challenge the administration officials who were trying to put a good face on a bad situation.

As a wire service reporter for UPI for many years at the White House, privileged to ask the first or second question at presidential news conferences, I gained a reputation for giving no one—presidents or press secretaries—any quarter. As far as I was concerned, they had to be accountable, and they had to explain their policies and actions to the American people.

That is why I was amused when President Bush-2 said, "I'm the commander, see. . . . I do not need to explain why I say things. That's the interesting thing about being the president. [I] don't feel I owe anybody an explanation."

Bush-2 also told Brit Hume, a Fox News correspondent, that he did not get his news from newspapers, radio, or TV. "The best way to get the news is from objective sources. And the most objective sources I have are people on my staff who tell me what is happening in the world." From a man who only tolerates yes-men/women around him, that was a hoot.

Since Bush-2 took office, I have worked for Hearst Newspapers as a columnist and am no longer a wire service reporter. Therefore, I am no longer eligible to ask the first question at a news conference. However, Bush keeps me off his A-list so I can't ask any questions at all.

While he began to hold more news conferences in his second term, most were limited to only a few reporters. Seldom did they rock the boat. Early on, the questions were predictable and easily fielded by Bush, who had been prepped in advance. But as time went on, reporters—nagged by the public—began to ask more penetrating questions of the president and pressed the press secretary even more aggressively. Bush was easily irritated when pushed to the wall with a question. Nor did he abide leaks in his highly secretive, locked-down administration.

"Helen was one of the first reporters to aggressively question the President's approach to Iraq," Fleischer wrote. He printed the following exchange and several others that occurred before and after the war began.

On February 12, 2002:

Helen: Is the President ready to go to war in Iraq?

Ari: Helen, as the President said in his State of the Union, the President is prepared to take whatever action is necessary to protect the United States, protect our allies, and to protect peace internationally. And I can assure you that no decisions have been made beyond the first phase of the war on terrorism. The President has been very plainspoken with the American people about the need to fight the war on terrorism wherever terrorism is. And he's focused right now on Afghanistan, but the President has been very clear that time is not on our side because of the threats posed by nations and terrorists against the United States.

Helen: Does he know of any connection with the current fight against terrorism by Iraq? Does he have any evidence?

Ari: Well, when the President referred to the axis of evil and identified North Korea, Iran and Iraq, what the President was referring to is their—not only their support of terrorism, which is plain—they are on the State Department list of terrorist states, but also their development of weapons of mass destruction, their willingness in the case of those nations to export technology and material and provide weapons of mass destruction. And the President does fear the marrying of any of these nations with terrorist organizations.

Helen: Well, we have weapons of mass destruction and we don't permit inspection.

Ari: Helen, if you're suggesting that there's a moral equivalent of the United States' success in keeping the peace for sixty years with our weapons and the actions of terrorism, I would urge you to reexamine that premise. I see no moral equivalence.

On May 1, 2002:

> Helen: Ari, what is the President's rationale for invading Iraq? I have been reading stories every day on preparations, no set plan yet, I admit, but anyway, all of the senior administration officials talk all the time, including the President, about a change of regime. What is the rationale for that?
>
> Ari: Well, Helen, the President does believe that the people of Iraq, as well as the region, would be better off without Saddam Hussein in charge of Iraq.
>
> Helen: A lot of people would be better off in a lot of places.

Fleischer went on to say that Congress had passed the Iraqi Liberation Act, calling for regime change, during the Clinton administration.

On September 4, 2002:

> Helen: Beyond his opinion that the world will be better off, did he [the President] present any concrete evidence of Iraq on the verge of nuclear planning, nuclear bombs, or any other thing that would really be different from what Israel has today?
>
> Ari: First of all, I don't think it's fair to compare Israel to Iraq.
>
> Helen: Why not? It's the only nuclear power in the Middle East.

On January 6, 2003:

> Helen: At the earlier briefing, Ari, you said that the President deplored the taking of innocent lives. Does

that apply to all innocent lives in the world? And I have a follow-up.

Ari: I refer specifically to a horrible terrorist attack on Tel Aviv that killed scores and wounded hundreds. And the President, as he said in his statement yesterday, deplores in the strongest terms the taking of those lives and the wounding of those people, innocents in Israel.

Helen: My follow-up is why does he want to drop bombs on innocent Iraqis?

Ari: Helen, the question is how to protect Americans, and our allies and friends.

Helen: They're not attacking you.

Ari: . . . From a country.

Helen: Have they [the Iraqis] ever laid a glove on you or the United States in eleven years?

Ari: I guess you have forgotten about the Americans who were killed in the first Gulf War as a result of Saddam Hussein's aggression then.

Helen: Is this revenge? Eleven years of revenge?

Ari: Helen, I think you know very well that the President's position is that he wants to avert war, and that the President has asked the United Nations to go into Iraq to help with the purpose of averting war.

Helen: Would the President attack innocent Iraqi lives?

Ari: The Iraqi people are represented by their government. If there was regime change, the Iraqi . . .

Helen: So, they will be vulnerable?

Ari: Actually, the President has made it very clear that he has no dispute with the people of Iraq. That the American policy remains a policy of regime change. There is no question the people of Iraq . . .

Helen: That's a decision for them to make, isn't it? It's their country.

Ari: Helen, if you think the people of Iraq are in a

position to dictate who their dictator is, I don't think
that has been what history has shown.
Helen: I think many countries don't have that decision,
including us.

On March 14, 2003:

Helen: Ari, will you ask the President for me and for
many, many others, has he really weighed the human
cost on both sides, starting a war to go after one
man?
Ari: Helen, this is not a war to go after one man. This
is a war. If this is a war [it started five days ago] to go
after one regime led by Saddam Hussein that possesses
weapons of mass destruction that can take the lives of
millions. That's why the United States called on Saddam Hussein to disarm. It is because Iran-Iraq possesses weapons of mass destruction and that is the core
of the issue. They have not disarmed.
Helen: How do you know they do [have WMD], when
they haven't been discovered? We've had inspections,
and so forth, and many other countries have weapons
of mass destruction, including us.
Ari: And under Resolution 1441, Saddam Hussein was
compelled by the United Nations Security Council to
immediately, without conditions, and without restric-
tion, disarm. He has not done so.
Helen: You haven't found anything yet in the . . .
Ari: That doesn't prove he doesn't have it, Helen. It
just proves he is able to hide it.

Fleischer concedes in his book that the administration may
have been wrong about Saddam Hussein's "capabilities, but we
weren't wrong about his intentions."
I also have had my moments with Fleischer's successor, the

unflappable Scott McClellan, who also stayed on message, no matter what.

On May 25, 2005:

> Helen: The other day—in fact this week, you [McClellan] said that we, the United States, [are] in Afghanistan and Iraq by invitation. Would you like to correct that incredible distortion of American history—
> Scott: No. We are—that's where we are currently—
> Helen: In view of your credibility [which] is already mired? How can you say that?
> Scott: Helen, I think everyone in this room knows that you're taking that comment out of context. There are two democratically-elected governments in Iraq and—
> Helen: Were we invited into Iraq?
> Scott: There are democratically-elected governments now in Iraq and Afghanistan, and we are there at their invitation. They are sovereign governments, and we are there today—
> Helen: You mean, if they asked us out, that we would have left?
> Scott: No, Helen, I'm talking about today. We are there at their invitation. They are sovereign governments—
> Helen: I'm talking about today, too.
> Scott: —and we are doing all we can to train and equip their security forces so that they can provide for their own security as they move forward on a free and democratic future.
> Helen: Did we invade those countries?
> Scott: Go ahead, Steve [with your question, referring to Steve Holland, Reuters White House correspondent].

Those were the days when I longed for ABC-TV's great Sam Donaldson to back up my questions as he always did, and I did the same for him and other daring reporters.

Then I realized that the old pros, reporters whom I had known in the past, many around during World War II and later the Vietnam War, reporters who had some historical perspective on government deception and folly, were not around anymore.

Journalists also indicated that if they dissented from the official administration line, they could be considered unpatriotic in a jingoistic atmosphere.

I honestly believe that if reporters had put the spotlight on the flaws in the Bush administration's war policies, they could have saved the country the heartache and the losses of American and Iraqi lives.

It was past time for reporters to forget the party line, ask the tough questions, and let the chips fall where they may.

CHAPTER 10

FOREIGN CORRESPONDENTS IN IRAQ— DÉJÀ VU ALL OVER AGAIN!

There wasn't a reporter in the White House pressroom who did not know for nearly two years that President Bush could not be deterred from going to war. The spin, the deliberate government leaks, the disinformation—all were a piece of the Bush administration's news management.

War is hell.

Operation Iraqi Freedom is no exception to that observation, and it is particularly hellish because it is an unnecessary war that has cost thousands of lives of innocent civilians, American and foreign military, and journalists. The United States had invaded because Iraq's leadership by Saddam Hussein was depicted as a threat to our security. The "threat," those much discussed weapons of mass destruction (WMD), was never discovered. That rationale was far-fetched—Iraq against a superpower? And an Iraq crippled by economic sanctions at that.

There doesn't seem to be a "light at the end of the tunnel" in this three-year conflict any more than there was in the Vietnam War, until the Communists declared victory in 1975 with the loss of more than fifty-eight thousand U.S. troops, and fatalities in the millions of Vietnamese, military and civilian. Some four dozen American and allied journalists were killed in Indochina.

The Committee to Protect Journalists reported in mid-2005

that forty-one journalists had been killed in the Iraq War: thirteen in 2003; twenty-three in 2004; and five to date in 2005. In the last two years, the dead reporters were mostly Iraqis, who were able to venture closer to battle sites because they resembled the general populace.

Around the world, the committee says fifty-six journalists were killed in 2004; eighteen had died by mid-2005. There were 399 journalists killed in the decade 1992–2001 on foreign assignment.

The contrast between American war reporting and depth of coverage in Vietnam, Laos, and Cambodia as opposed to that in Iraq is overwhelming. In Vietnam, a press badge or a reporter shouting "Bao chi!" (press, media) often carried authority in a conflict. In Iraq, it often is a hindrance or just plain dangerous to be identified with the media from any country.

Correspondents and photographers in Vietnam were able to climb on a helicopter and fly to Da Nang, where a press center had been set up by the military, or Da Lat, in the Central Highlands, or the southern delta, for eyewitness accounts. Certainly, Vietnam was a dangerous and difficult place to live and work as all war zones are, but freedom of movement was possible in most areas of South Vietnam, especially when the U.S. military still ran the show. In Baghdad, the Green Zone, where the U.S. command operates, was designed to be safe from attack, but even that section was infiltrated by insurgents and hit by weapons fire on several occasions.

As General Tommy R. Franks, former commander in chief of the U.S. Central Command, who had been in both wars, said in his book *American Soldier,* "In Vietnam, we essentially knew the boundaries of where the enemy was and where we could go. This is not the case in Iraq where the insurgents seem to be widely spread out and active with few boundaries." U.S. and allied troops had to learn to be jungle fighters in Vietnam. In Iraq, urban warfare has taken its toll with roadside bombs and "suicide bombers" favored as the weapons of choice for the resistance in Baghdad and other populated areas. Kidnappings and beheadings were a constant threat earlier in the Iraq war. In Vietnam, Buddhist monks regularly committed self-immolation to make an antiwar statement, but when they killed themselves, they didn't take fifty innocent civilians with them to martyrdom.

Ironically, it was the urban warfare Bush-1 warned about that kept the United States from going on to Baghdad after the victory in Kuwait in the first Gulf war, but his son told an interviewer he listens to a higher "Father."

As I think back to the buildup to the invasion of Iraq, I was startled that so many reporters and photographers at the Pentagon and the White House supported the war. The reporters displayed little of their usual skepticism about the upcoming war and bought the spin. As the years have gone on and the casualties have mounted, editors and publishers now report having difficulty recruiting enough staff to cover the war. Within two years of war without an exit strategy and no plans for one, the zeal and enthusiasm to be a war correspondent in Iraq evaporated. It diminished in Vietnam, too, at first after the 1968 Tet offensive, and then markedly after the U.S. military pullout began in the early seventies.

The *Los Angeles Times* reported (5/9/05) that journalists were becoming more aware of the dangers of war reporting. Networks such as CNN, ABC, CBS, and NBC all agreed to follow the guidelines established by the News Security Group in 2000. Under the agreed code, the *Times* said, "assignments to war zones or hostile environments must be voluntary." A growing number of journalists were reluctant to make risky trips to Iraq, which the New York–based Committee to Protect Journalists rated as one of the five most dangerous places in the world for reporters. The *Times* article quotes Alan Philips, foreign editor of Britain's *Daily Telegraph,* as saying, "We still have volunteers, but I would say it's harder" to get staff to go there.

Before the war, there was no doubt that American reporters,

mainly from Washington, were gung ho, exuding excitement and exhilaration to be chosen by their respective news agencies to become foreign correspondents in a war zone where the action meant bylined stories every day if you lived to write them.

In Vietnam, many reporters, such as David Halberstam, Neil Sheehan, Malcolm Browne, Joe Galloway, Peter Arnett, and others, made a journalistic name for themselves covering the war. It will be interesting to see what fame will emanate from the Iraq debacle. But I doubt that many reporters will get close enough to tell the human-interest story. It's just not that kind of war. Reporters venture outside the highly protected Green Zone at their own risk. It is Russian roulette.

In retrospect, it is astounding that the media unquestioningly accepted the false justification of an administration clearly bent on military aggression in the name of removing a dictator running a country that had not attacked us. The same thing could be said for North Vietnam, a small agrarian nation that didn't attack us either, but at that time the spread of Communism loomed large around the free world, and by treaty we were committed to defend South Vietnam. The military and congressional "hawks" on the war argued that if Communism took hold in South Vietnam, it would be only a matter of months before most of Southeast Asia would be overrun. South Vietnam did fall to the Communists, but the "domino effect" never happened.

"Those who cannot remember the past are condemned to repeat it," said the early-twentieth-century philosopher George Santayana.

On March 19, 2003, at the White House and the Pentagon there was an atmosphere of enthusiasm and excitement when the invasion of Iraq began. Only the exact timing was a surprise.

After the start of the bombing, a pool of reporters and cameramen were ushered into the Oval Office. Asked how he felt about starting a war, Bush said, "I feel good." Still, most of the media present didn't challenge Bush's decision or ask him how he could justify the invasion especially when so many of our allies, with the exception of Great Britain and Australia, had expressed their reservations about the war.

At the Pentagon, Rumsfeld dominated the news briefings in the run-up to the war, bragging about the "shock and awe" missiles that were about to be targeted on the Iraqis. Rumsfeld became a media rock star in that period, strutting and swaggering. The reporters accepted this without demanding evidence of an Iraqi threat against the world. Rumsfeld could say anything without fear of contradiction or even challenge at that time. Who in the press was going to rock the boat? We were going to war.

During the Vietnam War and in other wars, journalists were viewed as noncombatants and had some immunity. This time around, Americans, no matter their status, were as vulnerable as any soldier fighting in Iraq.

Wall Street Journal reporter Daniel Pearl was among the first of many correspondents who was to pay the ultimate price in the war that knew no front lines. David Bloom, an NBC White House correspondent, died of an embolism in the tank in which he was riding and columnist Michael Kelly, editor-at-large for *Atlantic* monthly, was killed when his Humvee overturned. Many more were to follow.

In a letter to the editor of the *Washington Post* (6/18/05), Aidan White, general secretary of the International Federation of Journalists in Brussels, Belgium, criticized the U.S. and Iraqi military for the secrecy surrounding the deaths of journalists.

"Journalists in the United States, led by the Newspaper Guild–CWA and the American Federation of Radio and Television Artists, called on President Bush to ensure that all media deaths are properly investigated," White said. "The reports on the killings—and in some cases, no reports have been filed—follow the same pattern: secrecy about the detail and nature of the report; a failure to examine all the evidence; insensitive shrugs of regret and exoneration of responsibility of U.S. personnel at all levels of command. . . . It is inappropriate for the military to investigate itself without any independent or judicial review. Perhaps most worrying, the absence of credible inquiry leads to speculation about the targeting of journalists by U.S. soldiers."

White concluded that unless U.S. authorities address concerns about "the paltry response to media deaths, the anger and sense of injustice felt by many in journalism will remain."

Under a newly devised Pentagon system called embedding, reporters were allowed to travel with the military units and become eyewitnesses to the opening shots of the war. They saw the horrors of the killing fields and lived in the same discomfort as the GIs, with constant fear and little sleep.

Before being assigned to military units, the embedded journalists had to sign a contract restricting when and what they could report. The details of military maneuvers could not be described in detail, and the reporters agreed not to write about classified information or future missions, which might endanger the lives of the troops. Some Iraqi reporters, hired by the U.S. or British news agencies, were imprisoned, accused of helping the "insurgents." The military in Baghdad often refused to provide any information about their whereabouts and cause of jailing. Further, the commander of a unit could declare a "blackout" on satellite communications to keep a correspondent from broadcasting. Similar restrictions have been required in other war situations, although advanced technology was not present earlier. In the Vietnam War, film had to be shipped by air or boat and there were no cell phones.

The embedding system was devised by the Pentagon in response to criticism that the media were given limited access to the military during Desert Storm, the Gulf war in 1991, and the incursions in Grenada and Panama. Reporters had accompanied troops in other wars, including Vietnam, but not in such large numbers—six hundred were embedded at the start of the Iraqi invasion.

The *New York Times* (3/23/03) also said, five days after the war started, that some reporters were allowed to sit in on secret briefings, but were barred from filing stories.

Marvin Kalb, former CBS news correspondent currently attached to the Shorenstein Center on the Press, Politics and Public Policy at Harvard University, said embedding was a gutsy, risky call for Rumsfeld, designed to enlist the support of the American people.

Michael Hedges, veteran war correspondent for the *Houston Chronicle,* who covered Desert Storm, Bosnia, and the start of the Iraq invasion, said he and his colleagues initially believed the administration's claims of the presence of weapons of mass destruction.

"I wouldn't have lugged around forty-five pounds of chemical protection if I hadn't believed that they would find WMD," Hedges said. One of the first correspondents to reach Tikrit, Saddam Hussein's hometown, Hedges said he was surprised at the strength of the insurgency. He originally thought that the only Iraqis who would fight back would be the Saddam loyalists. That was not the case as the months of war and bloodshed have proven. Many resisting the U.S. presence were Iraqis with support from other Arab nations.

The number of correspondents traveling with the troops dwindled after a few months in Iraq as the practicalities of keeping the war covered became expensive for publications and television networks already feeling an economic crunch from competition. Agreed-upon tours of duty ended, and it became increasingly dangerous for Western journalists and photographers to be there.

Ann Cooper, director of the Committee to Protect Journalists, told the *Los Angeles Times,* "There's been a change from the era of macho reporting when it was not cool to appear frightened. Now there's a greater sensitivity to safety issues."

Loren Jenkins, foreign editor for National Public Radio, said, "Our approach is pretty basic. No story is worth your life. We'd rather have no story than a dead correspondent."

In general, the embedding concept, at least for a limited time, seemed to satisfy the media. There was some hesitation and some speculation that embedding was another way of saying "in bed with," where the correspondents would be co-opted as military cheerleaders, but that apparently did not happen.

By and large, the reporters who remained were not a critical lot, and their news agencies were more concerned with keeping them alive than criticizing the war. The cable television companies admittedly shied away from showing gruesome film from Iraq. The government did not have to censor cable networks; they censored themselves in a protective military/press complicity. The Bush administration had it made, early on. As the war went on, however, and the casualty numbers began to rise, the figures began to have an impact.

Before leaving office as secretary of state, Colin Powell said, "We did not expect it would be quite this intense this long."

Michael Hedges said there was great danger for journalists covering this war because of the enormous firepower of new weapons and the difficulty of understanding the enemy and its religious factions.

From a journalist's standpoint, Hedges said that embedding was different from filing copy in a "pool report." He said he was often beaten on his own exclusives in other conflicts because he had to share the story first with other reporters, filing his pieces after they'd sent their dispatches. He felt that embedding was better for the reporter looking for exclusivity. For instance, there was a story of the reporter embedded in a truck convoy that crossed a bridge over a shallow creek. The bridge collapsed and the hapless journalist lost his computer, tape recorder, and cell phone in the water. He filed his story from memory some hours later.

Many correspondents and cameramen struck out on their own, were not attached to any action unit, and were called unilaterals or independents, trying to find their stories without military affiliation.

Author and teacher Kate Webb, who had a distinguished career as a combat correspondent in Vietnam and was captured for twenty-three days in Cambodia, said, "The real and present danger of Iraq-style embedding lies in the flip side—the U.S. military saying that they cannot be responsible for the safety of the independent media."

One correspondent described it as treating the "embeds" like official reporters and the independents as unofficial and therefore outside the information or interview loop.

Ms. Webb noted that the writing and reporting of a good seasoned reporter will not be affected by being embedded, but he or she can waste weeks of valuable time and observation if put into an inactive unit and unable to move. The danger for "green, inexperienced reporters" is that they can see only through one lens, she observed.

Even Rumsfeld acknowledged that the embedded reporters were seeing only "slices of the war in Iraq."

"It is one slice and it is the totality of that," he said. "This is what this war is about."

Yes, indeed, it was Rumsfeld's war without any uplifting glory for the United States. However, deception in a democracy often catches up with the perpetrators.

As Joe Galloway, a Knight Ridder Newspapers military columnist and author of *We Were Soldiers Once—and Young*, pointed out, the Pentagon spun a story about the death of army ranger Pat Tillman, the former NFL football star. Tillman, who gave up the spotlight to become a soldier, was described by the military as a hero killed in battle. In fact, it was later admitted that he was killed by American bullets, or friendly fire.

Galloway also recalled the false stories about the dramatic rescue and heroism of Private Jessica Lynch that were "foisted on reporters during the opening days of the attack on Iraq."

She was described as having "fought to the last bullet before being wounded and captured." The truth was, Galloway wrote, Private Lynch was injured when the vehicle in which she was riding crashed and she was knocked unconscious. She never fired a shot.

The aftermath showed better people, more interested in the truth, including the Tillman family despairing of their late son being used as a poster boy to sell the war when he was killed by his own colleagues. Lynch gave interviews telling the true story of her capture and good treatment in an Iraqi hospital.

When a public outcry forced the controversial Office of Strategic Influence (OSI), or office of disinformation, to be disbanded, Pentagon officials made no bones about the fact that they would find other ways to use misleading information and plant stories as a military tool. Galloway wrote that the decision of commanders in Iraq "to combine information operations, psychological operations, and public affairs into a single strategic communications office" was troubling.

An example of mixing news and psychological information (psyops) occurred during the 2004–5 Falluja campaign when a military spokesman appeared on CNN and dramatically announced that troops had marched on the Iraqi city. In fact, the offensive did not kick off until three weeks later.

Mark Mazzetti, writing in the *Los Angeles Times,* said that the announcement was "carefully worded" as an elaborate psychological operation "intended to dupe insurgents in Falluja and allow U.S. commanders to see how guerrillas would react if they believed troops were entering the city."

The question of using false information has been controversial in the wartime Pentagon. However, the CNN incident was similar to countless other deceptions used throughout history by armies to deceive their enemies, Mazzetti wrote, quoting Pentagon and national security officials.

Galloway, who covered the Vietnam War thirty years ago, recalled the Five-O'Clock Follies, where he said "lies and spin were dispensed along with the facts" by Americans and South Vietnamese. The Follies were the daily media briefings held at the appointed hour in Saigon (now Ho Chi Minh City), which largely became a joke because of the discrepancies between what the media observed and how the military and the U.S. embassy wanted it reported. During those years, the media had access to firefights, rocket attacks, and support bases, which made military dissembling difficult to maintain.

Vietnam was the first war to be televised, and in his first interview after leaving the White House, President Johnson told CBS-TV anchorman Walter Cronkite that television killed his ability to seek reelection. He referred to the newscasts coming across the TV screens in American living rooms every evening that incited nationwide protests against the war.

In their book *The Press,* Geneva Overholser and Kathleen Hall Jamieson note that the Vietnam War was uncensored with a freedom of movement and expression "rarely accorded correspondents.

"The American military men in the field said the war was being fought foolishly and being lost, and the American people were being misled by cooked numbers and inappropriate optimism," Overholser and Jamieson said. Iraq was déjà vu all over again.

The authors disposed of some myths about the Vietnam War: that there was hostility between the correspondents and the military and that the media lost the war. The authors said polls showed that public support for the war in Vietnam had turned long before the press delivered up the "hot pictures" and the disillusions that set in after the 1968 Tet offensive.

Reporters in that era were quite detached from their own patriotic instincts when it came time to cover a story. And they did not bury the bad news, which no doubt churned up the antiwar protests. The media showed the graphic photographs and told the heartbreaking stories. As a reader or viewer, you were right there.

News reached the United States more slowly in the Southeast Asian conflict. Reporters were thousands of miles away and communications were unreliable. Computers were in their infancy and Teletype machines, now obsolete, transmitted news around the world. South Vietnamese President Nguyen Van Thieu kept UPI and AP Teletype machines in his bunker office at Independence Palace in Saigon with large paper maps of the country's military areas (I Corps, II Corps, etc.) pinned to the walls with thumbtacks, an unsophisticated operation.

Television news hadn't begun twenty-four-hour news cycles, and foreign media coverage was limited. Communist Radio Hanoi broadcast combat casualty figures from both sides— and they were usually correct. This is very different from the Pentagon, which for a long time said, "We don't count Iraqi casualties."

After the 1968 Tet offensive, a turning point in the Vietnam War, the military and official Washington, stung by criticism, began to turn against the reporters on the scene. Much to President Johnson's distress, the correspondents were describing a no-win war unless North Vietnam was bombed "back to the stone age," as the late General Curtis LeMay suggested. Some columnists, such as the late Joseph Alsop, assured LBJ that if he bombed North Vietnam for six months, the war would be over. Senator Barry Goldwater, a conservative Republican from Arizona and presidential candidate, suggested building a giant fence along the demilitarized zone to keep the North and the South permanently separate. The Vietnam War hurt both Johnson and Nixon, who looked for ways to extricate the country from its Cold War folly.

Thirty years later, as the war in Iraq dragged on, controlling the news became state-of-the-art at the White House and the Pentagon. The Arab world saw so much more of the war than Americans, who were denied the true picture by the Bush administration and press organizations who were afraid to challenge the White House or the Pentagon. The U.S. pressure against Aljazeera, which had an audience in the Arab world of 40 million viewers and was reporting a graphic aspect of the war that annoyed American officials, caused the interim Iraqi government to banish Aljazeera from Iraq coverage. *Al Hawza,* the newspaper run by the Shiite rebel leader Muqtada al-Sadr, was shut down by the U.S. military, which gave the insurgency a new cause. Al Arabiya was also temporarily shut out, but they resumed broadcasting by reporting the news as American officials requested. So much for freedom of the press.

The widely reported story of the Pentagon's ban on photo coverage of soldier coffins arriving nightly from Iraq and Afghanistan at Delaware's Dover Air Force Base finally awakened the public to the manipulation of war news. Administration officials said the ban began with former President Clinton and tried to attribute the policy of prohibiting distribution of photos of military coffins to empathy for the grieving families. The Pentagon and White House said piously they wanted to protect the privacy of families in mourning, but many of the relatives would undoubtedly have wanted the world to pay last respects with them. There was one slipup when the computer Web site the Memory Hole filed a Freedom of Information Act request for pictures of the coffins arriving at Dover. The Air Force Air Mobility Command inadvertently granted the request, so the world was able to see a selection of 361 images taken by Defense Department cameramen. In fact, a *New York Times*/CBS News Poll showed that 62 percent of Americans polled said photos of the military-flag-draped coffins should publicly be shown. Unfortunately, most news agencies and other outlets did not challenge the strict rules and went along, as usual, with the administration. The military insisted that photographs only had a proper context at the gravesite, but that was obviously a fallacious excuse. In 2005, Ralph Begleiter, a former CNN correspondent and journalism professor, sued the Pentagon—with the backing of the American Civil Liberties Union—to gain release of photos of flag-draped coffins returning from the war.

As they did after 9/11, many newspapers and TV stations ran tributes to the fallen heroes so they would not be forgotten. Local media have also made an effort to cover memorial services for soldiers and followed up with stories about grieving families and hardship. American publications have also made an effort to run substantially more photos of Iraqi casualties simply because the dead and wounded count is higher for them than for U.S. and allied troops.

In my many years as a White House correspondent, I have learned that some photographers are the best reporters I know. They see things, sometimes in a split second, that elude even perceptive reporters. I have had the privilege of knowing many photographers who know what is going on, know the players, but they also know that their pictures can most powerfully tell the story.

War coverage by photography began during the Civil War when Alexander Gardner's pictures of Confederate soldiers killed and wounded at Antietam showed the tragedy of war. Mathew Brady displayed Civil War photos at his galleries in New York and Washington, but the average American didn't see them.

In the American wars that have followed, including the ongoing combat in Iraq, photographers have captured stunning and poignant images from the battle zones. Yet, it has always been a personal struggle for many battle photographers whether to take, or publish, photos of the dead and wounded.

During the Spanish-American War, technology and travel had advanced enough that photographers could transmit their photos to newspapers by ship, but some considered it disrespectful to take pictures of the dead.

In World War I and the early months of World War II, U.S. military censors blocked most photos of American losses, according to James Rainey, writing in the *Los Angeles Times*. That meant few pictures of the dead or wounded. Even pictures of bombed-out tanks, jeeps, and other equipment could be censored by the military on the grounds that it would harm morale on the home front.

Susan Moeller, author of *Shooting War: Photography and the*

American Experience of Combat, said the morale issue changed in 1943 when President Franklin D. Roosevelt and the War Department decided that Americans needed to see the true risks and costs of war.

After restrictions were lifted, pictures of the dead and wounded began to appear regularly, especially in *Life* magazine, which noted that "words are not enough" to show the tragedy of war.

Rather than offend the public, the photos helped to synthesize U.S. opinion in support of the war, Moeller, a University of Maryland journalism professor, said.

Photojournalism really came into its own during the Vietnam War, when photographers had the freedom and access, thanks to the military, to roam around Vietnam taking extraordinary pictures where they found them. It was not pictures of American GIs or U.S. casualties that became the iconic images of the Vietnam War, Rainey notes. Instead, photos of a Buddhist monk immolating himself, a naked girl fleeing a napalm attack, and the head of South Vietnam's national police executing a Viet Cong prisoner with a shot to the head—those were the permanent images of that war that helped to turn the tide against it in the American psyche.

When the U.S. military invaded the Caribbean island of Grenada in 1983, the Reagan administration left reporters and photographers behind. That fueled a backlash and agreement from the military in the 1991 Persian Gulf War to allow limited access to a pool of media who would share their findings with other news outlets.

The arrangement allowed a minimal view of the fighting, but photographers protested their limited access and military control of their film until it was often too old for publication.

Rainey said that American newspapers and magazines have printed few pictures of American casualties in Iraq. Photographers and editors who made the decisions agreed that the main reason was logistical. With a handful of photographers at any time covering a nation the size of California, a probing camera was usually absent when a guerrilla attack occurred. Scenes of roadside bombings typically showed only a burned-out armored vehicle.

On other occasions, the military interceded to block pictures of the dead and wounded being rushed to hospitals, or sometimes the photojournalists would decide on their own to withhold the most gory pictures. U.S. television also delivered greatly reduced imagery of war casualties. A George Washington University survey of two thousand TV news segments found that the war had been "sanitized" and rendered "free of bloodshed," especially in cable TV operations.

To quote an old Chinese proverb, one picture *is* worth a thousand words.

Chapter 11

The Greatest American Journalists of Our Times

I believe that the journalists of the past—including print and electronic media, as well as photographers—were more dedicated to the profession than those now. And many today—perhaps too many—laid down their lives to get the story in Iraq. But call it nostalgia or just my observation, but something has been missing in the spirit and attitude of journalists, who seem to lack the same sense of humanity the job has required for greatness.

I do believe that American journalism had its heyday in the twentieth century. That is because some of the most historic and world-shaking events occurred during those volatile years. It produced the most brilliant and perceptive correspondents the country has ever known.

Many more have come along in recent years—but the electronic media and instancy of the news delivery cannot match the eloquence and in-depth reporting of the print journalists. In those good old days before television, the story was the thing. Journalists had a certain amount of anonymity.

Television has transformed journalists into personalities, who become more important than their stories. There is less and less ability to tell the story objectively, and the viewer is the loser.

The reporters at the turn of the twentieth century were not refined: they were lucky if they had a high school education. They were often first hired in their teens as copyboys (later copygirls)—long before journalism interns were given the opportunity to learn the business from the ground up.

Essentially, the "copy kids" were gofers who cut copy from Teletype machines, ran to newsstands to buy competitive newspapers, and brought cups of coffee to acerbic editors.

Nothing could replace the excitement, however, of the insistent two-bell ring on a Teletype machine announcing a bulletin or the proverbial police reporter as in Ben Hecht's *The Front Page* calling to say, "I've got a story that will break this town wide open." Or the other cry from reporter to dictationist: "Hello, sweetheart. Get me rewrite."

Romanticized, but so frequently true in the lives of the old-time reporters. They would have a pint of booze on the floor or in the bottom desk drawer, or something more hazardous, as did the legendary Aggie Underwood, city editor of the *Los Angeles Herald-Express,* who carried a gun in her purse to ward off corrupt politicians in the Old West.

These reporters did not have master's and doctorate degrees, but they had an innate sense of news—a figurative nose for news—and a great sense of integrity about the profession.

They earned measly salaries with overtime pay a fantasy until the American Newspaper Guild was founded in the late 1930s to establish pay standards for the industry. Many of these professionals did not win the coveted Pulitzer Prize, but they brought glory to their work by performing a vital role, bringing news to the American people to keep them informed.

Like him or not, and he certainly had his detractors, one must recognize H. L. Mencken, the turn-of-the-century iconoclastic Baltimore journalist with an elegant writing style. Mencken wrote for the *Baltimore Morning Herald* and the *Baltimore Sun.* His acerbic column, "The Free Lance," ran in hundreds of newspapers. He died in 1956. Mencken was an editor, a journalist, and a linguistic lover of the language. One of his best-known books is *The American Language.*

In "H. L. Mencken: The Joyous Libertarian," author Murray Rothbard said Mencken's guiding passion was individual liberty. He quoted Mencken as saying he was "against any man and any organization which seeks to limit or deny that freedom."

Controversial is the mildest label you could hang on Mencken. He was accused of being anti-Semitic, a bigot, a hater of minorities, and contemptuous of politicians and hypocrites.

Mencken described his early days as a reporter in his book *Newspaper Days* as "the maddest, gladdest, damnedest existence ever enjoyed by mortal youth." Those were the days when he was spending time "at large in a wicked seaport of half a million people, with a front row seat at every public show."

When he covered the so-called Monkey Trial in Dayton, Tennessee, in which John Scopes was on trial for teaching Darwin's theory of evolution, Mencken had to be protected by the local sheriff. Mencken did not endear himself to the local population when he referred to them as "yokels," "morons," "half-wits," and "hillbillies." He also referred to the silver-tongued politician William Jennings Bryan, who led the crusade to ban teaching Darwin's theories in the schools, as an "unmitigated ass," likening his sincerity to that of the showman P. T. Barnum.

Mencken felt that all government was evil and all government must necessarily make war upon liberty. He believed in the complete freedom of thought and speech, in the capacity of man to find out what the world is made of, and in the "reality of progress."

Dorothy Thompson, who was born in 1894 in Lancaster, New York, and died in 1961 in Portugal, was viewed as one of the two most influential women in America along with First Lady Eleanor Roosevelt in 1939 when war was breaking out in Europe. Ms. Thompson took controversial stands and backed the underdog. She wrote a column, "On the Record," three times a week and appeared as a magazine writer and commentator on NBC radio.

Ms. Thompson became head of the Berlin Bureau of the *New York Evening Post* in 1925. She was expelled from Nazi Germany in 1934 when she infuriated Adolf Hitler with her dispatches warning Americans against the rise of Nazism.

In 1934, Ms. Thompson wrote, "As far as I can see, I was really put out of Germany for the crime of blasphemy. My offense was to think Hitler was just an ordinary man, after all. That is a crime in the reigning cult in Germany which says Hitler is a Messiah sent by God to save the German people. . . .

"To question this mystic mission is so heinous that, if you are a German, you can be sent to jail. I, fortunately, am an American, so I was merely sent to Paris. Worse things can happen."

She also declared in 1935, "No people ever recognize their dictator in advance. He never stands for election on the platform of dictatorship. He always represents himself as the instrument of Incorporated National Will. . . . When our dictator turns up, you can depend on it that he will be one of the boys, and he will stand for everything traditionally American. And nobody will ever say 'Heil' to him, nor will they call him 'Führer' or 'Duce' [Mussolini's title]. But they will greet him with one great big, universal, democratic, sheeplike bleat of 'Okay, Chief!'"

Ms. Thompson said, "Only when we are no longer afraid do we begin to live." She was not afraid of controversy and supported the establishment of a Jewish nation in Palestine, but later became anti-Zionist and pro-Arab in her writings.

She was the inspiration for Katharine Hepburn's role in the movie *Woman of the Year* in 1942. She was described as an American Cassandra, seeing World War II coming to Europe. She led the way for many women journalists and became a role model for her generation.

Journalism is a calling, and it certainly was for Martha Gellhorn, one of the outstanding women war correspondents, who covered wars from the Spanish civil war in the late 1930s to wars into the late 1980s. She was tough and brave, taking incredible chances to get a story, lying in the mud next to Republican soldiers in Spain as they fought the Fascists led by Generalissimo Francisco Franco. Gellhorn had gone to Madrid with a knapsack and $50. She spoke no Spanish.

For five years she was the third wife of novelist-correspondent Ernest Hemingway, but resented being identified that way. Both she and Hemingway saw the Spanish civil war in the mid-1930s as a prelude to another world war. Hemingway immortalized it in his classic novel *For Whom the Bell Tolls.*

The poets, writers, and journalists who supported the International Brigades on the Republican side also believed it was the last chance to halt the slide toward World War II. Instead, it was the prologue so many had feared.

During the D-day landings in World War II on June 6, 1944, Gellhorn posed as a stretcher bearer, subjecting herself to grave danger. She also flew with British pilots on bombing raids over Germany and tagged along with the Allied troops when they liberated Dachau.

Gellhorn did not fit the stereotype of a hard-bitten reporter. She was a tall, gregarious, glamorous blonde with a great sense of compassion and justice. Caroline Moorehead, author of the Gellhorn biography *Gellhorn: A Twentieth Century Life,* wrote, "Martha was more committed than almost any journalist of her generation to promoting the cause of oppressed people."

Born in St. Louis into a wealthy family, she left Bryn Mawr College in her junior year to pursue a career in journalism, beginning with reading galleys for the *New Republic* in New York. She later reported for the *Albany Times, St. Louis Post-Dispatch,* United Press, *Vogue, Collier's, Atlantic* monthly, and *The New York Times Magazine.*

In going to Spain to cover the civil war, she wondered whether journalistic objectivity was required for writers witnessing atrocities carried out by the Fascists and the Republicans. The fighting was immortalized in Pablo Picasso's great war mural *Guernica,* which hangs in the Prado museum in Madrid.

Gellhorn was the only woman correspondent in the front lines of the Spanish civil war. Even as she got older and retired in Wales, she never lost her fighting spirit or sense of indignation. She believed it was her job to continue writing and to set the record straight "in the hopes that at some point or other, somebody couldn't absolutely lie about it."

Call it a sentimental nostalgia, but I feel I was tremendously lucky to have met in passing the most dedicated, fearless, insightful journalists of my time. They were not superficial. They were in the business because they loved it. They burned with a combination of adrenaline and outrage against injustice in society.

"You meet such interesting people," reporters were told so many times. How true. Great reporters do not sequester themselves in ivory towers; they know nothing can replace being "there." So many journalists and photographers through the years have lost their lives by insisting on being there, especially at the front in too many wars of recent times.

This country has been blessed with outstanding journalists who were in the right place at the right time, from the major big-city publications to the weekly newspapers in rural areas. Each had an important place in the community, and each served a purpose in rallying the citizenry to the things that mattered to them.

Today's women broadcasters owe a lot to trailblazer Pauline Frederick, who, fortunately for the country, did not take the advice of her boss, who told her to find another career because "radio doesn't like women." In that era, the 1930s, women were told their voices were too high-pitched for radio. Frederick defied that description, and her low-key voice was described as "mellifluous." Frederick was born in Gallitzin, Pennsylvania, and died at the age of eighty-four in 1990.

She started her career as a newspaper reporter before finding her niche as a highly respected commentator on international affairs. She worked for both ABC and NBC television networks, becoming NBC's top correspondent at the United Nations. She was awarded nearly every honor in broadcasting, including the Alfred I. duPont Commentator Award in 1953 for "exemplifying the best traditions of news commentary." The citation said that the pioneering journalist "avoided the slickness, automatic orthodoxy, and superficial sensationalism characteristic of much news commentary." TV commentators today should learn by her example.

She was the first woman to be elected president of the United Nations Correspondents Association. Ms. Frederick also received scores of honorary degrees. She was a broadcaster for National Public Radio only months before she died.

A stellar war correspondent was Marguerite Higgins, also a blond glamour girl, who gave her male colleagues a run for their money for her gutsy reporting in World War II, Korea, and Vietnam.

Higgins was born in Hong Kong to American parents. Her family moved to the United States when she was only two years old. She earned her undergraduate degree in journalism at the University of California and her master's in journalism at Columbia University.

She was hired by the *Herald Tribune* in 1942 and fought for an overseas assignment. In 1942, she was sent to London by her newspaper and covered the final months of the war in London, France, and Germany. She was with the Allied troops when they liberated the concentration camps at Dachau and Buchenwald.

She was a trailblazer for women journalists, particularly in the 1950s, when her star shone brightest. In Korea, she maneuvered her way to the front by begging jeep rides with GIs, or when that failed, with the army's top brass. One of her greatest triumphs was to prevail on General Douglas MacArthur to rescind his order barring women correspondents from the front battle lines.

She was the first woman reporter in Korea, having hitched a ride on MacArthur's plane when he flew from Japan to South Korea at the start of the war in 1950. And she was with the marines when they landed in Inchon, two hundred miles behind the North Korean lines, in September 1950.

She defied her employer, the *New York Herald Tribune,* and remained in South Korea when the newspaper sent its star reporter, Homer Bigart, to cover the war. The newspaper ordered her back to work in the Tokyo bureau. Furious at being replaced by Bigart, Higgins stayed in Korea and competed for stories against him, a rivalry that kept Washington abuzz during the war. The rift was the talk of the town.

By journalistic standards, Bigart was a far better and more professional journalist than Higgins. However, she copped all the honors for her work: a Pulitzer Prize for international reporting; Woman of the Year award from the Associated Press; and her book *War in Korea* became a best seller.

Higgins was sent to Vietnam by the *Herald Tribune* in 1953 and covered the defeat of the French at Dien Bien Phu. She displayed remarkable courage in Vietnam and narrowly escaped injury many times. Ultimately, she became disillusioned with the war, saw its futility, and documented her reasons in her book *Our Vietnam Nightmare,* published in 1965, the year that President Lyndon B. Johnson began a full-scale war in Southeast Asia.

Ms. Higgins died in 1966 of a tropical disease contracted in Vietnam. She was buried in Arlington National Cemetery. Her name is on the Vietnam Veterans Memorial wall in Washington, D.C.

Ernie Pyle, the Scripps Howard Newspapers reporter, covered World War II from the human side, as all war stories should be covered; his were so heartrending and powerful. Pyle wrote so vividly that GI Joe's personal problems on the battlefield were as real as cartoonist Bill Mauldin was able to depict them in his famed cartoons.

Pyle won the Pulitzer Prize for his reports on the human tragedy of war.

The weather-beaten, rugged-looking Pyle did not write about military policy or strategy. He left that to the pundits of the day. Instead, his stories dealt with the dirty clothes, wet shoes, dreams, hunger, anger, and courage of the men he was covering.

He identified with the underdog and wrote, "They are mud-rain-frost-and-wind boys. They have no comforts and they even learn to live without necessities. And to the end they are the guys that war can't be won without."

Pyle was born on a farm in Dana, Indiana, and had nearly completed four years at Indiana University when he was offered a job on the local newspaper in 1923. He moved on to the *Washington Daily News,* a Scripps Howard newspaper, and within a few months became its managing editor. He detested desk work and soon became a roving reporter and columnist for United Features, a newspaper syndicate owned by Scripps Howard, in 1938. In 1942, Pyle was sent to cover the Nazi blitz of London with the nightly aerial bombing raids from over the English Channel from the European mainland.

Pyle set the formula and the tone for war correspondents to follow. In the words of the poet John Donne, "Any man's death diminishes me, because I am involved in mankind." Pyle made that clear, and there has been no one to match him.

During the war, Pyle covered North Africa and parts of Italy and later the Pacific, where his luck ran out. He was killed by a Japanese gunner on a tiny island off the coast of Okinawa while covering the Army's Seventy-seventh Division. The GIs with whom he had bonded and related built him a simple monument. The plaque read, "At this spot, the infantry division lost a buddy, Ernie Pyle. 18 April 1945."

Lest I appear to gush, well, so be it. I believe that Merriman Smith, head of the White House bureau for United Press International, and my late husband, Douglas Cornell, a White House correspondent for Associated Press from 1940 to 1971, were the two most outstanding wire service reporters ever to cover the presidency.

You will never read more factual, straight copy on some of the most critical historical events of our times than what these two correspondents filed daily. There was no slant, no bias, no innuendo, in their stories. They wrote what they knew and never injected themselves into the report. To sum it up, they delivered pure, unadulterated news to the people, and they would never have it otherwise.

Smith, known to everyone as Smitty, was an extraordinary reporter who covered the White House like a blanket. Nothing was too trivial to write about, from the overpopulation of squirrels on the front lawn to reports critical to the nation and the world. His instruction to me was "Write everything."

He could handle them all—the lighter moments with wit and enthusiasm, the crises with the speed and accuracy they merited. He was the idol of the pressroom, a cantankerous one who could charm any audience with his embroidered stories. Smitty was a raconteur par excellence and a performer, sophisticated with no small ego, and yet he had a tremendous understanding and sympathy for the people he covered. He was undoubtedly one of the most colorful reporters that ever came down the pike in Washington.

Smitty broke many stories about the presidents (he covered six) and their families. He also wrote a column, "Backstairs at the White House," filled with intimate tidbits about the denizens of the Executive Mansion, and he was a frequent guest on the popular late-night TV talk shows, hosted then by Jack Paar, Johnny Carson, and Merv Griffin. That was when TV discovered print reporters. A few years later newsmen and newswomen lost their anonymity and were featured on TV.

Smitty was the incomparable reporter's reporter, with his hat at an angle, breakneck dashes to telephones, and rapid-fire dictation from scribbled notes that only he could read.

When President Harry S. Truman announced the end of World War II, Smitty broke out of the door, slid across a table in the pressroom, and broke his collarbone. He got up and ran to the phone, dictating for an hour before acquiescing to the pain.

He covered political conventions and campaigns, such as Truman's famous whistle-stop tour in 1948 where crowds began to swell from one town to another. It was then that even the most cynical reporters began to think that Truman had a chance to win the election over the dapper Thomas E. Dewey, the Republican governor of New York.

I like the story about one reporter who had overstayed on the phone during the whistle-stop. He began running toward the train as it began to pull out of the station. He heard his laughing colleagues shouting, "Don't forget to write," before they pulled him on board.

This is a good example of reporters' sense of togetherness. They help each other, give their colleagues a fill-in on stories they have missed, and know it is all reciprocal.

Because Smitty showed up at Hyannis Port, Massachusetts, on election night in 1961, John F. Kennedy knew he had won the election. The story that made Smitty the most famous is one that has left the nation unhealed to this day—the assassination of President Kennedy by Lee Harvey Oswald in Dallas. Everyone alive at the time has been asked, "Where were you when Kennedy was shot?"—and everyone remembers.

Smitty was in the third car in the presidential motorcade in Dallas on November 22, 1963, when he heard three shots fired at the Kennedy limousine. He was a gun buff so he knew the sound of gunfire. He also had the acumen to sit in the front of the "wire car" provided to the White House press with its one telephone under the dashboard. After hearing the shots, Smitty began dictating bulletins to the UPI's Dallas office. He never relinquished the telephone, although the AP's reporter, Jack Bell, was beating on his back and head until the car arrived at Parkland Hospital.

Running into the hospital, Smitty saw Clint Hill, Jacqueline

Kennedy's chief Secret Service agent, pounding on the back of the limousine, and crying, "He's dead." Smitty ran into the hospital, located a telephone, and kept dictating when he learned that Kennedy's death had officially been announced by deputy press secretary Malcolm Kilduff. The news was flashed around the world by UPI teleprinters, leading with ten bells.

While he was on the phone, a Secret Service agent told him, "Smitty, the president is going back to Washington." He meant the president-to-be, Lyndon Baines Johnson. Smitty convinced a policeman to drive him and two other reporters, in a squad car, to Love Field, where Air Force One was preparing to take off. He boarded the plane with Sid Davis, a broadcaster, and Chuck Roberts of *Newsweek* magazine. Smitty was a witness to the swearing-in of President Johnson on the presidential plane in the presence of Jackie, in her pink, Chanel bloodstained suit, and a sorrowful Lady Bird Johnson, the new first lady, as well as several Kennedy and Johnson aides. Smitty won the Pulitzer Prize that year for his coverage of that tragic story.

I rank my late husband, Douglas Cornell of Associated Press, as one of the most talented wire-service reporters ever to come down the pike. I believe his colleagues from the early 1930s until 1971 would agree. He stood over a Teletype machine and dictated the end of World War II when Japan surrendered, no mean feat for any reporter.

Doug wound up in the doghouse with President Johnson when he wrote a captivating story about Johnson pulling his beagle's ears. Dog lovers were appalled and Johnson was reduced to sarcastic remarks about the number of White House reporters who were experts on "animal husbandry."

No story was too difficult or complicated for Doug. He was a beautiful, smooth writer, and he never deviated from the facts.

He was inspired by his English teacher in high school to become a journalist and went on to graduate from the University of Missouri School of Journalism in 1929. Doug was a newspaperman's newspaperman. He was trusted as a favorite for his fairness by presidents as far apart as Franklin D. Roosevelt and Richard M. Nixon.

Doug admired Roosevelt and was thrilled when he was allowed to bring his parents on FDR's campaign trail to meet the president. Nixon, as a California congressman, became acquainted with Doug when he covered the House of Representatives. He respected Doug for his professionalism and gave him a farewell party when Doug retired from the AP in 1971.

Doug's forte was the wrap-up story, the story coming from several directions, but all part of the piece. He had an uncanny talent for putting it all together in a brilliant opus. His byline was enough for an editor to grab the story and play it prominently on the front page. He was frequently tapped to write the final story on the death of a prominent politician . . . so much so that he was often teased as being Mr. Habeas Corpus.

He was quiet, but he was highly competitive, and he gave my boss, Merriman Smith, a run for his money when the AP and UPI were on minute-to-minute competitive deadlines. Doug and Smitty also were the best of friends. That's the way it used to be with wire-service reporters.

Doug could pick up a ten-page speech, race through it, pick up the telephone, and call in a bulletin lead to his office within seconds. I never knew him to miss the lead or first paragraph. They hardly make them like that anymore.

One cannot extol the outstanding correspondents of the last century without a deep bow to Edward R. Murrow, the great inspiration for broadcast journalists for decades to come.

He was born in a log cabin without electricity or plumbing on a farm near Polecat Creek near Greensboro, North Carolina, the youngest son of Quaker abolitionists. At the age of five, his family moved to Washington State near the Canadian border on Samish Bay. He excelled in a high school in nearby Edison, becoming head of the student body and a star on the debate team. He attended Washington State College, majoring in speech. He joined CBS in New York in 1935, remaining with the network until the end of his broadcast career.

During the 1938 Czechoslovakian crisis with Hitler, Murrow broadcast directly by shortwave radio from Prague, an event that made history. After that, Murrow and William L. Shirer, another famed foreign correspondent, teamed up to organize a European news roundup, which brought together correspondents from all over Europe for a single broadcast in 1938. It was the start of the CBS World News Roundup.

Murrow was sent to London before the outbreak of World War II, while Shirer remained in Berlin. Both of them electrified their radio audiences, Murrow with his direct radio programs from London during the Nazi blitz, and Shirer doing companion broadcasts from Berlin.

Murrow began to have problems with CBS Chairman William S. Paley when Murrow attacked Senator Joseph McCarthy's Communist "witch hunt" on the home front. Murrow and producer Fred Friendly, and their news staff, produced a devastating thirty-minute special entitled "A Report on Senator Joseph McCarthy," in which Murrow used excerpts from McCarthy's sinister speeches that caused a nationwide backlash against the Wisconsin senator and is often seen as a high point in television.

But Murrow also suffered from a fall in his ratings and conflicts with CBS and Paley, who lacked the stomach for the causes that the firebrand Murrow was stirring up, according to Friendly in his book *Due to Circumstances Beyond Our Control.*

· An exposé on the plight of migrant workers called "Harvest of Shame" was the last straw for the squeamish CBS honchos. Murrow quit CBS and accepted President Kennedy's offer to head the U.S. Information Agency.

A chain-smoker, Murrow died of lung cancer in 1965, better remembered than Paley or any colleagues of that period.

Murrow spoke profound words to express the true meaning of democracy and the need to preserve it. They apply so much today to an America that is polarized and fearful that its skepticism of White House statements may be construed as "unpatriotic."

In response to McCarthy, Murrow said, dissent is not disloyalty.

Murrow also spoke of the importance of citizens being free to speak their minds. "No one can terrorize a whole nation, unless we are all his accomplices," he said.

Murrow said in a broadcast on March 9, 1954, "We will not walk in fear, one of another. We will not be driven by fear into an age of unreason, if we dig deep in our history and our doctrine and remember that we are not descended from fearful men. Not from men who feared to write, to speak, to associate, and to defend causes that were for the moment unpopular. This is no time for men who oppose Senator McCarthy's methods to keep silent, or for those who approve. We can deny our heritage and our history, but we cannot escape responsibility for the result."

He also rebuked McCarthy, saying, "The junior senator from Wisconsin has caused alarm and dismay amongst our allies abroad, and given considerable comfort to our enemies. And whose fault is that? Not really his. He didn't create this situation of fear, he merely exploited it, and rather successfully. Cassius was right: 'The fault, dear Brutus, is not in our stars, but in ourselves.' "

Doris Fleeson was a political columnist who covered Washington for New York's *Daily News*. She was the sole permanent woman member of the press corps following President Franklin D. Roosevelt on his campaign tours. Her stinging columns were "must reading" for government officials. Ann Cottrell Free also was one of the few female reporters who broke into FDR's overwhelmingly male-dominated press corps and stayed the course.

Who can forget May Craig—the lady who always wore a hat—whose sharp tongue and Southern twang demanded the attention of presidents at their news conferences. She wrote for the Maine-based Gannett chain of newspapers and was a regular panelist on *Meet the Press* in the earliest days of the NBC-TV Sunday interview/talk show.

At one memorable news conference, perky May Craig asked President Kennedy, "What have you done for women lately?" His reply: "Obviously, Mrs. Craig—not enough."

There also was Ruth Gmeiner Frandsen of UPI, who was the first reporter to alert the UPI desk that the 1954 school desegregation decision was imminent, just before it was handed down by the U.S. Supreme Court. The decision was one of the most far-reaching in breaking down segregation in the country.

I would be remiss if I did not mention the late Sarah McClendon, who gave presidents heartburn and irritated the more sedate White House correspondents with her feistiness. She was my friend and I admired her courage and her outspokenness. She was a friend of the disadvantaged and those who had no forum for their legitimate causes and complaints.

She drew one of President Dwight D. Eisenhower's most famous responses when she asked what policy decisions Vice President Richard M. Nixon had participated in. Ike's devastating reply: "Give me a week and I'll think of something."

Born in Tyler, Texas, her father was the local Democratic Party chairman, and her grandmother and mother were leaders in a suffragist movement. At the age of three, Sarah marched with her grandmother in a suffragettes' parade, then came home, stood on the kitchen table, and repeated her grandmother's speech to her brothers and sisters. She worked for the Tyler newspapers and Texas's *Beaumont Enterprise* before joining the army in World War II in the first class of the Women's Army Corps. Sarah later served as a captain in the Pentagon's press relations division.

She made her mark at presidential press conferences, representing Texas newspapers.

Sarah was a great friend of the nation's veterans and took up their crusades for better health care, and when she told President Nixon that the Veterans Administration had defaulted on mailing veterans' benefit checks on time, they were in the mail within a few days. She died January 9, 2003, at the age of ninety-two. A room has been dedicated in her name at the National Press Club. The all-male institution "lost" her application for membership for sixteen years, but she was finally admitted to the club in 1971 when women were accepted as members.

No one could write like the peerless Pulitzer Prize–winning columnist Mary McGrory.

A prominent member of the post–World War II scene in Washington was I. F. Stone, better known as Izzy. Stone was a maverick leftist newsman who mined government committee reports and discovered gems for the public good. He was a loner and one-man editor, publishing a newsletter entitled *I. F. Stone's Weekly.* Throughout his career, Stone was a voice for a segment of society outside the mainstream media. Before he died in 1989, he was honored by the Washington press corps at the National Press Club for his courageous journalism.

Peter Lisagor, the Washington correspondent and bureau chief for the *Chicago Daily News,* was known as an incisive diplomatic reporter and a regular panelist on the political TV talk shows. A room has been named for him at the National Press Club.

James Reston, better known as Scotty, was born in Scotland; his family emigrated to the United States in 1920. Reston grew up in Ohio and went to work for the Springfield, Ohio, *Daily News* as a sports reporter.

He joined the AP in 1934 and moved to the London Bureau of the *New York Times* in 1939. During World War II, he took a leave of absence to establish a U.S. Office of War Information in London. He returned to the *Times* in 1945, making his superstar reputation in Washington as a national correspondent and columnist. His friendships with the Washington political elite gave him many exclusives. He won the Pulitzer Prize twice, in 1945 and 1957.

Reston's star shone in 1945 when he covered the international conference that paved the way for the gathering in San Francisco where the United Nations was founded. Reston persuaded the Chinese Nationalist delegate to give him documents on China's position, crucial at the time, and gave his news rivals a fit.

The *New York Times* learned about plans to use Cuban exiles for the Bay of Pigs invasion in 1961—President Kennedy urged the *Times* not to print the story on grounds of national security. The *Times* acquiesced, and when the invasion proved to be a debacle, Kennedy later said he wished the *Times* had printed it. Reston also learned early about the missile buildup during the Cuban missile crisis, but he agreed not to print the story because President Kennedy said the Soviets might take preemptive action if they knew the United States had discovered their plans.

Reston was accused of having too many friends in the Washington hierarchy, especially former Secretary of State Henry Kissinger, but no one doubted Reston's honesty, insight, balance, and sense of fairness.

Among the many remarkable reporters who covered the White House who had many exclusives in their day were my colleagues at UPI; Warren Rogers of Associated Press and the old *New York Herald Tribune,* who could give any competitors a run for their money on the diplomatic/Pentagon beat; and Robert Donovan, also a correspondent for the *New York Herald Tribune,* who covered the Truman whistle-stop campaign in 1948. Donovan, who later went to the *Los Angeles Times,* wrote *Conflict and Crisis: The Presidency of Harry S Truman, 1945–1948,* one of the best biographies on the former president.

Journalist Peter Arnett, a New Zealander, won a Pulitzer Prize covering the Vietnam War for AP. He knew that you had to be *there* and to see with your eyes the events that you wrote about. Arnett reported one of the most famous quotations that emerged from the Vietnam War: "We had to destroy the village in order to save it."

Arnett's career has had its ups and downs. Wars have been his specialty, and because of that he has accumulated a number of enemies in high places.

After his long stint with AP, he went to work for the Cable News Network (CNN), and he became a household name for his outstanding live coverage of the first Gulf war, sticking his head out of his hotel window to report on the first U.S. bombs falling on Baghdad. He ran into trouble with Washington when he reported that a baby-milk factory had been bombed. American officials insisted it was a biological weapons factory. There has never been any proof that it was not a milk factory, but Arnett was officially repudiated.

When the Gulf War ended, Arnett continued to broadcast for CNN, but on June 7, 1998, a script he had not reviewed was thrust into his hands to broadcast, accusing U.S. army commanders of using sarin nerve gas in a top-secret operation called Tailwind during the Vietnam War. The report accused Tailwind participants of using the gas against defectors who were hiding in a village in Laos. The Pentagon disclaimed the report and CNN fired Arnett. He later was fired by NBC and MSNBC after he gave an interview on state-controlled Iraqi TV outlets saying that the U.S. war plan for Iraq had failed and the war planners had misjudged the Iraqi opposition. What a joke, considering that the U.S. government had set up and financed TV outlets in Iraq for propaganda purposes. Arnett's series of bosses could not stand the heat from the administration and had neither the patience nor the courage to determine whether what he was saying had merit. Arnett was "shocked," as he put it, to be put out to pasture so many times by major news organizations who refused to support a controversial figure.

Arnett had one credo: "I present both sides and report what I see with my own eyes." Arnett did not try to fix the facts as many in the Bush-2 administration did. His holy grail as a reporter was the truth as he saw it. Obviously that was not acceptable to his skittish television employers.

There aren't many journalists whose names crop up as possible presidential candidates, but Missouri-born Walter Cronkite, described for a time as "the most trusted man in America," was often mentioned as a possible leader for the country.

But, he was a newsman. It was his great love and he spent a lifetime in journalism. Cronkite began working for his University of Texas college newspaper, but switched to United Press during World War II, advancing to Moscow bureau chief for the wire service. After the war, radio and TV began to draw on trained print journalists to give authenticity to broadcasting. Cronkite got in on the ground floor. Even as a young man, Cronkite came across as avuncular with gravitas, a voice of authority. He was hired by two CBS affiliates before advancing to the network. Later, he helped develop the *CBS Evening News,* where he spent nineteen professional years as anchorman.

He gave memorable broadcasts during the space shots, including the moon landing. Cronkite broke down in tears when he announced that President Kennedy was assassinated, but kept broadcasting.

Cronkite was courageous and often stuck his neck out in defense of freedom of the press. His personal memoirs, *A Reporter's Life,* were published in 1996. Cronkite retired in 1981, saying he was pushed out by CBS news management, which was more interested in infotainment than hard news. He still narrates PBS specials as of this writing.

Always a hard-news print journalist at heart, Cronkite concluded his book by questioning TV's influence on the political process: "The major problem is simply that television is an inadequate substitute for a good newspaper."

I have almost run out of superlatives to express my admiration for investigative reporter Seymour "Sy" Hersh, a correspondent with a tremendous conscience. Would that there were more of his caliber. He continues to expose Americans who should have represented the highest standards of human behavior, but did not. For their misdeeds, we are all to blame. We Americans let these terrible things happen.

Hersh gained his first major recognition in 1969 when he

revealed the My Lai massacre and its cover-up during the Vietnam War. On March 16, 1968, a platoon led by Lieutenant William Calley killed hundreds of civilians—an entire village of elderly men, women, children, and babies, herded into a ditch and machine-gunned. A memorial at the site of the massacre, never rebuilt as a village, named 504 victims, ranging in age from eighty-two to one. News of the atrocity exploded in the United States and gave even more impetus to the growing antiwar movement. For his brilliant reporting, Hersh won the Pulitzer Prize.

More recently, Hersh, who worked for both UPI and AP before moving on to the *New York Times* Washington bureau, has been in the forefront in disclosing the brutal, sadistic mistreatment and torture of prisoners held by the U.S. military in Abu Ghraib prison near Baghdad. The stories, written for *The New Yorker* magazine, backed up by photos shown worldwide, shocked America, but not enough to make President Bush-2 reaffirm America's pledge to adhere to the Geneva Conventions on Humane Treatment of Prisoners of War. The compassionate conservative Bush and his top aides said they did not support the use of torture, but they never did anything to stop it. When commission after commission revealed the abuse of prisoners, the administration made sure that no one in the upper chain of command would be found responsible. The only persons blamed for the horrors were low-ranking officers and one woman general in the reserves.

Seymour Hersh is a hero in the annals of American journalists. He exposed the administration's deceptive shenanigans before the invasion of Iraq and its covert operations in Iran. Richard Perle, former chairman of the Defense Policy Board Advisory Committee, and a rabid neocon who pushed relentlessly for war with Iraq, said Hersh was the "closest thing American journalism has to a terrorist."

Of course Hersh antagonized the Pentagon and the White House, but the public owes him a tremendous debt of gratitude for putting the spotlight on their clandestine operations, and alerting us to their intentions, not to mention the shameful policies that tarnished all Americans.

These journalists are not only the giants in our business who deserve praise and respect, but they are among the better known and perfectly exemplify the finest journalistic standards of an era now past.

Other, more contemporary journalists I admire are Ron Cohen, Washington Bureau chief at UPI, Wesley Pippert, David Wiessler, Lori Santos, and Steve Gerstel. They are unsung heroes who have worked in the news vineyards among some of the most intrepid and dedicated journalists of modern times. I must include Dan Rather of CBS, Tom Brokaw of NBC, and the late Peter Jennings of ABC. Sam Donaldson of ABC stands out to me as a straight reporter on television, as well as Cokie Roberts and Loren Jenkins with National Public Radio.

The current columnists I admire are William Raspberry and E. J. Dionne of the *Washington Post,* and Paul Krugman, Frank Rich, Bob Herbert, and Maureen Dowd of the *New York Times.*

Epilogue

I believe that the media has to do some soul-searching to determine its role in the future after a rocky start in the twenty-first century. Perhaps it is unrealistic, but I would like to see a return to what I consider the ideal values in journalism and less focus on entertainment and financial gain. Justice William O. Douglas wrote, "The press has a preferred position in our constitutional scheme, not to enable it to make money, not to set newsmen apart as a favored class, but to bring to fulfillment the public's right to know."

Newspapers and other media outlets, including radio and network and cable television, should examine themselves and decide who they are and how they want to be perceived. There is no question the media has invited skepticism from the public through the misdeeds of some charlatans. While the press scandals have been a setback for journalists, they have been dealt with quickly by editors and publishers, several of whom got caught in the cross fire. There is a tacit code of ethics in the profession, and credibility is the key among the standards. As I conclude this book, I would like to offer some suggestions and observations to future journalists to reinvigorate the profession.

Although I approach journalism as someone with more than sixty years' experience, and every day is a learning experience for me, I have observed that the new generation of reporters have little knowledge or institutional memory of either their country or their profession.

To some extent, that is understandable, but what is not acceptable is to be uninformed about American history and the Constitution, especially the Bill of Rights. Young reporters often do not have much knowledge of D-day, the turning point in World War II; the long-draining Vietnam War; the Pentagon Papers case; the Watergate scandal and the relevance of Deep Throat; the Cold War and its end; the space race; and many other fairly recent history-making developments. It is extremely important to understand these events in order to put today's news into proper historical context. My advice to potential reporters and editors is, read, read, read! It is a truism that a person who doesn't read is no better off than a person who can't read.

Good journalism still is being taught in the "j-schools," and the profession remains a drawing card for thousands of students nationwide.

A reporter's report card is in the newspaper dailies, and there is no salvation on a major blooper. Nor is there much tolerance for controversy in newspaper hierarchies. Publishers and editors should back up their staffs instead of running for cover when a story is challenged—especially if they know the facts to be right.

The lack of fight by the media against the manipulation of government officials who play the fear card or imply that legitimate criticism is disloyal or unpatriotic astounds me. Cable News Network (CNN) pulled back on a documentary on the struggle over intelligence by insiders. Some news agencies held off announcing that women marines were killed in Iraq for fear of offending the public and the government. Gruesome photos have been archived rather than made available to newspapers after brave photographers in Iraq took enormous risks to produce them. The censorship is subtle and often self-imposed. It is a way of hiding unpleasant facts—but the role of the press is to report the truth.

Future journalists should abhor unsourced news and be on guard against the government's use of actors who pretend they are reporters and cover the news with a pro-administration slant, a favorite ploy of the Bush-2 team. And, broadcast stations that accept government handouts and videos should make their sources clearly known. Otherwise, they are participating in the deception.

A press pass should be worn only by legitimate reporters who adhere to the journalist's creed, a relentless search for truth without fear or favor. Also, journalists should be constantly aware that defamatory stories can ruin lives and reputations. Therefore, extreme caution and good judgment should be used in exposing the private lives of public figures.

To say that journalism has changed is to put it mildly. The proliferation of the Internet affects how the public receives news. Consumers expect rapid news updates. Journalists must keep up as well, often using the Internet in their arsenal of research tools.

The Internet further parses the news-seeking public. There are generational differences that cannot be ignored. Corporate news conglomerates, Washington insiders, and world leaders alike now give consideration to a continuum and combination that ranges from paper to broadband.

The Internet also increases the temptation for sloppy journalism. It's easy for even the most seasoned reporter to substitute an online search for investigative reporting. There is no replacement for nurturing stories, courting sources, and tracking down leads. The Internet can play a role in the hunt, but it is not the soup-to-nuts solution to a good story.

Progress has given birth to a double-edged sword. I've talked at length about news management in this country. In countries lacking the free press of a democracy, the most extreme example of news management is government propaganda. In the past, such nations' citizens have relied on the airwaves and word of mouth to learn the truth. The digital age can bring news via the

Internet to those previously deprived of truthful accounts. In a paradoxical way, the other edge of the sword is the uncensored Internet for all. The public should know the difference between the mainstream media and those practicing "journalism" over the Internet.

A phenomenon known as the web log, or blog, emerged on the World Wide Web slightly less than a decade ago. Blogs are online journals. Because such journals frequently link to news items, the boundaries between sanctioned news outlets and public opinion are becoming blurred. At present, the majority of people don't read blogs. In fact, a study by the Pew Internet & American Life Project puts the number who do at 25 percent, but this percentage is likely to grow considerably over time.

I've read that the number of blogs is approaching a million. This number is so astoundingly high that we should ponder what it represents to society as well as the mainstream media. Society has changed; we're too fast-paced for old-fashioned social gatherings. Young people, especially, are connected all the time. I think those who enjoy talking around the watercooler or chewing the fat at local socials have found a virtual format for such communities of opinion. And from what I've read, trained journalists who blog love the freedom of unedited opinions. Opinion it is—unfettered stream of consciousness, a marketplace of rumors, instantaneous feedback and discussion, a bully pulpit for all. Journalism it's not.

The horse is out of the barn. Blogs are the new opinion poll. Blogs, therefore, affect how the news is covered. Blogs and bloggers can lead credentialed journalists to news stories. Bloggers are not journalists and should not undermine the mainstream press. Bloggers are not deserving of reporter's privileges—to think so is ludicrous.

Suzanne Condray, professor of communications at Denison University, is a keen observer of the changes in communications. She says, "Clearly, the press has struggled to claim its role as an information source as the Internet has become a primary information source. But like broadcasting was to print, the Internet remains yet another messenger, and what it still needs is investigation, clarification, and interpretation. The public spends less and less time with traditional sources of news, while there is a proliferation of alternative cable channels. And even public broadcasting is on the chopping block. But that is precisely the point. Change occurs in the midst of tensions which groan with futility. Just as whistle-blowers stepped forward in the 1970s and the courts responded, such is happening as those whose sense of ethics demands that the inside traders and corporate barons cease to rob our citizenry and when the SEC steps forward and the courts impose fines and sentences, we witness that change."

We also witness change when "students wince when they see footage from the Vietnam era and realize that reporters aren't showing them the same scenes of war today," Condray said. "Fifty years ago, it took a few folks some time to realize that what they were being told was worthy of being questioned, but little by little that occurred. The press played a demonstrable job bringing an isolated event in one part of the country into homes of folks thousands of miles away. The press did so as well in helping to bring an end to the U.S. commitment in Southeast Asia a world away. Again, what was necessary was an investigative voice, a few individuals willing to see the merits of citizenry rather than systems and others recognizing the power of constitutional rights as a step forward."

Condray went on to say, "We must remember that the college students of today are the children of the parents of the 1970s. In short, seeds invariably grow when nurtured, and I believe the press is at a crucial juncture in recognizing its heritage and the power of its voice, if it can but take that challenge and adapt to new technologies, new voices, and different circumstances reflected in this generation. Although I don't see young people today embrace the traditional press, I see in their idealism . . . the potential for change in the coming years."

When people say to me, "You can't believe everything you read in the newspaper," my reply is "Ninety-nine percent of the time you can count on it."

The new dimensions and burdens on journalists often boil down to money. Those running the newspapers and radio and television stations are ever more conscious of keeping costs down and keeping their shareholders happy because competition among the media outlets is fierce and becoming more so. That isn't the way it used to be, but now the owners of the vast communications empires seem to care less about the news and more about entertainment, which brings in the cash.

The new technology has spawned a new form of communications previously unknown and has opened up a whole new world of information, available at the click of a mouse. But what has not changed in a democracy is the raison d'être of journalism, the people's right to know.

One of the most outstanding and enlightened interviews I conducted while writing this book was with Tom Johnson of Atlanta, Georgia, who reigned at the top of newspaper and television empires for decades and remains an avid enthusiast of journalism. If anyone has seen it all, it is Johnson, a former deputy press secretary in the Lyndon B. Johnson White House. Tom was no relation to the late president, but he might as well have been. The president treated the bright, attractive young man as the son he never had.

Tom also worked under press secretaries George Reedy and Bill Moyers in the 1960s. Then he went on to become the publisher of the now defunct *Dallas Times Herald* and later the *Los Angeles Times,* excelling at both jobs in the print media. Now retired, Tom was tapped by entrepreneur Ted Turner to become the chief executive officer of CNN in its infancy.

I will never forget when Turner dropped into the White House pressroom when CNN was a start-up. He poked ABC-TV's Sam Donaldson in the chest and told him, "We will bury you." It seemed far-fetched at the time, and Donaldson laughed, but

CNN and the other cable outlets have given the major commercial networks a run for their money.

As much as I extol the news, it's not called the newspaper business for nothing. During most of the twentieth century, newspapers were independent, not owned by the giant conglomerates, and often family-owned, such as the Dix newspaper, radio, and TV chain in Ohio, which is still operated by the fourth and fifth generation of Dixes.

It's a different story now. Big corporations such as Gannett own a hefty share of newspapers, and the TV networks are owned by corporations that have other interests. General Electric is the parent company for the National Broadcasting Company, Viacom owns the Columbia Broadcasting System, and Disney owns the American Broadcasting System.

And there's the rub. Tom Johnson bemoans the new emphasis on the "bottom line" instead of "good journalism." He deplores the heavy focus on earnings, profitability, and the purchase of independent newspapers. He noted that the new leaders in the industry put a greater emphasis on earnings and their responsibility to the shareholders.

Tom offered great praise to his former employers Turner and Otis Chandler, former publisher of the *Los Angeles Times,* who were dedicated to journalism and were "fierce protectors" of their editorial employees while remaining independent of outside pressures. He also saluted the Sulzberger family, owners of the *New York Times,* and the Graham family, publishers of the *Washington Post.*

Tom had some great moments in running CNN. His most brilliant achievement was during the first Gulf war when he initiated satellite coverage and created instant war reportage.

He said he "took an enormous amount of heat" when he tried to present the Palestinian side of the Middle East dispute as well as the Israeli point of view. There also were the right-wing denigrators who labeled CNN "the Clinton News Network" and "the Castro News Network," he said.

The essence of a good news story still is the five W's: who, what, where, when, and why. It also should give both sides of a controversy a fair shake so that the reader will understand the issues.

Once upon a time, the newspapers told the story first and even put out special editions when the breaking news demanded big, bold headlines like "War Declared." Newspapers now play second fiddle to broadcast outlets, which go on the air in a matter of seconds with "breaking news." All the TV or radio correspondent needs to do is pick up a microphone or a telephone or make a fast run to the cameras. It is then left to the newspapers to tell the story in depth and flesh out the details with interpretation.

I think that the essential approach to what newspapers are supposed to be about was laid out in the Scripps Howard handbook, which was first issued in 1948. It should be the gospel for all newspapers and said:

"We have no politics, that is, in the sense of the word commonly used. We are not Republican, not Democrat, not Greenback and not Prohibitionist. We simply intend to support good men and condemn the bad ones, no matter what party they belong to. We shall tell no lies about persons or policies for love or money.

"It is no part of a newspaper's business to array itself on the side of this or that party. The newspaper should simply present the facts the editor is capable of obtaining concerning men and measures before the bar or the public and then, having discharged its duty as a witness, to leave the jury in this case, the public, to find the verdict."

Scripps Howard was founded by E. W. Scripps, who said his greatest contribution to journalism was to create United Press, which later became United Press International. In laying down his creed, the handbook also said:

"We believe in orderly social progress, we distrust concentrations of power. We believe in the democratic way of life, although we understand that unrestricted democracy would be anarchy, and that society must be governed by rules. We believe in a government of laws, rather than by men. We believe the individual is paramount to the state and the purpose of government is to serve society, not society serve the government. We believe it is the duty of the strong to protect the weak and to champion the cause and support the hopes and aspirations of the underprivileged and inarticulate. We do not believe in a limited and restricted view of a free press. We believe in the spirit, not merely the letter of the Bill of Rights. We consider it a grant of freedom to the people; and we feel as journalists we are the trustees of this freedom."

I worked as a wire-service reporter for UPI for more than fifty years, and I do believe that it was the most reliable way to keep the American people and the world informed—just the facts presented in the fairest way. I also believe that the demise of UPI as a strong competitor to the Associated Press was hurtful to the practice of good journalism.

"Just the facts, ma'am" was the mantra at UPI. An adjective, an adverb, or a verb that projected an opinion was blue-penciled. If there is such a thing as objectivity, we came closest to it and always strived for it. I still stand in the greatest admiration of editors who were so perceptive they would not even let a subtle slant slip by them. After all, we were serving newspapers all over the world, newspapers and broadcasters of different shades of opinion. They deserved—and were paying for—a straight story.

Accuracy also is the essence of a news story, and that takes a lot of fact-checking and "being there." As the saying used to go, "If your mother says she loves you, check it out."

I now write an opinion column for Hearst Newspapers, which gives me a wide berth to express myself on the issues of the day, but I must say that I still believe that straight news reporting is the best journalism and most rewarding to the reader. Not that it is not a great privilege and fun to spout my opinion after so many years of restraint. It also has its pitfalls as I have learned every day when I read my e-mail from strong dissenters. If they wrote merely a tough rebuttal, that would be fine, but I find that the critics are not satisfied to tell you how wrong you are, they must vent personal attacks to make their point. And from that aspect, I find it all sad. A good, honest debate is the essence of democracy.

Or as Adlai Stevenson, twice-defeated Democratic contender for the presidency in the 1950s, said, "Democracy is great because it is safe to be in the minority."

But to denigrate and demonize the media just to spew anger and frustration is cause enough for a response of pushing the delete button on the computer. Of course, it is not all one-sided. There also are encouraging messages on the Internet from strangers who are happy when the mainstream media wake up and stop giving the White House and other government spokes-men a free pass on their "spin."

If the people are more cynical about the media, they should be even more so about the people in government who could not care less about credibility. Trust in government has eroded for good cause when leaders take the country into war under false pretenses and carry out the nation's business in secrecy, but there would have been more transparency if the press had been more vigilant.

Throughout this period of great disappointment with the media, I must say I take my hat off to the political cartoonists and those who produce the daily comic strips. They were on the money, courageously telling the truth in humorous satire. They showed the courage and persistence I find lacking in many reporters as we begin a new century. Garry Trudeau was out-standing in depicting the cynicism of preemptive war in Iraq and the tragedy of its wake. He and his fellow cartoonists put truth ahead of government spin.

In welcoming to the White House the incoming first lady, Hillary Rodham Clinton, the presiding first lady, Barbara Bush, pointed to the press corps and said, "Avoid this crowd like the plague. And if they quote you, make damn sure they heard you."

Some reporters do make the grade as friends of a president and his family or keep their sources inside the White House that have been cultivated on the campaign trail. They still can write critical stories, and sometimes they do, which strains the friendship with presidents who thought the correspondents were always on their side. Fairness and accuracy are all that any government or industry officials can ask for, and they do deserve that.

We are the guardians of the people's right to know, not of transient administrations who misuse and abuse their power, often to muzzle the press. It was Abraham Lincoln who said, "Let the people know the facts and the country will be safe."

I believe that, and I believe that is the purpose and promise of journalists in the twenty-first century and beyond.

INDEX

Index

Hearst, William Randolph, 9
Hearst Newspapers, 146, 199
Hedges, Michael, 159, 160
Hemingway, Ernest, 173
Herbert, Bob, 190
Hersh, Seymour, 188–90
Hicks, Nancy, 122–23
Higgins, Marguerite, xx, 175–76
Hill, Clint, 179–80
Hinchey, Maurice, 130, 132
Hinckley, John, Jr., 47
Hispanics, 115, 116
Hitler, Adolf, 172, 182
"H. L. Mencken: The Joyous Libertar-
  ian" (Rothbard), 171
Hoffman, David, 144
Hogan, Thomas, 88, 104–5, 109
Hoover, J. Edgar, 18
House of Representatives, U.S., 23, 25,
  108, 181
House Un-American Activities
  Committee (HUAC), 98
Houston Chronicle, 137, 159
Hoy, 113
Huffington, Arianna, 145
Hume, Brit, 146
Humphrey, Hubert, 61, 74
Hussein, Saddam, 54–55, 85, 138, 139,
  141, 143, 147, 148, 149, 150

I. F. Stone's Weekly, 185
Indochina, 153
Information Agency, U.S., 182
insurgency, 154, 158, 159, 165, 187
Intelligence Identities Protection Act
  (1982), 88
Internal Revenue Service (IRS), 76, 113
International Brigades, 173
International Federation of Journalists,
  157
International News Service, 29
Internet, xiv, 1, 193–94
  newspaper sites on, 113, 115, 122
  print content utilized on, 116–17
Interstate Commerce Commission, 125
In Touch Weekly, 116
investigative reporting, 13–16, 17–19,
  21–22

Iran, 20, 80, 147, 150
Iran-contra scandal, 20–22, 48, 49–50
Iranian hostage crisis, 71, 80
Iraq, Kuwait invaded by, 85
Iraqi Liberation Act, 148
Iraq War, xviii, 60, 73, 135–52
  Aljazeera and, xix, 60, 164–65
  changing rationales for, 137–39,
    143–44, 145, 148, 150, 153, 156
  editorial page bias and, 136, 140
  inevitability of, 142, 143–44, 153,
    156
  journalists killed in, 154, 157
  lies and misinformation leading up to,
    16, 40, 54–55, 85, 103, 136, 137–39,
    189, 200
  limited photojournalist access in,
    167–68
  media blackouts in, 158
  press complicity in, 135–38, 139, 140,
    145, 155, 156–57, 160
  press self-examination in coverage of,
    136, 139–43
Israel, 148, 149

Jackson Citizen Patriot, 90
Jaffe v. Redmond, 106
Jamieson, Kathleen Hall, 136, 163
Janeway, Michael, 1
Japan, 34, 176
Jay, John, 58–59
Jefferson, Thomas, xxii, 9, 111
Jenkins, Loren, 159, 190
Jennings, Peter, 190
John F. Kennedy Profile in Courage
  Award, 93
Johnson, Lady Bird, 31, 43, 180
Johnson, Lyndon B., 17, 31, 32, 40,
  41–43, 92, 94, 164, 176, 180
  favoritism shown by, 71–72
  press relations of, 41–42, 69–70,
    71–72, 163
Johnson, Tom, 196
Johnson administration, 63, 69–73
Jones, Paula, 23
journalistic ethics, 1–12, 135, 191
  anonymous sources and, 88–90, 96,
    135, 136

journalistic privilege, 97–100, 103
  Supreme Court rejection of, 99–100,
    105
Jungle, The (Sinclair), 14–15
Jupiter Courier, 3
Jurgensen, Karen, 5
Justice Department, U.S., xviii, 22, 29,
    75, 108

Kalb, Marvin, 159
Kay, David, 55, 138
Keith, Damon, xviii
Kelley, Jack, 2, 5–6, 12, 88
Kelly, Michael, 157
Kennedy, Caroline, 38
Kennedy, Jacqueline, 32, 38, 179–80
Kennedy, John F., 23, 27, 29–30, 31, 32,
    37, 38–40, 61, 68, 182, 186
  assassination of, 179–80, 188
  as news manager, 63, 64
  press relations of, 64–65, 67–68, 184
  public relations practiced by, 65–66
Kennedy, Robert F., Jr., 130
Kennedy, Rose, 32
Kennedy administration, 58, 63–69
Kerry, John, 7, 131–32
Kessler, Glenn, 106
Khrushchev, Nikita, 61
Kilduff, Malcolm, 180
Kinsley, Michael, 144
Kissinger, Henry, 17, 45, 75, 91, 186
Klein, Herbert G., 43
Knight Ridder, Washington bureau of,
    143
Koehler, Robert C., 139–40
Koestler, Arthur, 19
Korean War, 175–76
Krugman, Paul, 190
Kumar, Martha, 8
Kurtz, Howard, 140
Kuwait, 82, 155

Laitin, Joe, 40
Lance, Bert, 22
Laos, 154
Lavin, Carl, 90
Leaders (Nixon), 76
leaks, leakers, 66, 93–97, 146

national security and, 76–77
  as news management tool, 59, 62,
    153
  presidents as, 64, 74, 87
  see also sources; whistle-blowers
Lebanon, 20
Lehnert, Eileen, 89–90
Leiberman, Jon, 7
LeMay, Curtis, 164
Lewinsky, Monica, 23, 24–25, 50–51, 83
Libby, I. Lewis "Scooter," 105
Libya, 22
Life, 167
Limbaugh, Rush, 131
Lincoln, Abraham, 59, 111, 201
Lindley, Ernest K., 9
Lippmann, Walter, xxi, 9, 117–18
Lisagor, Peter, 185
Lockhart, Joe, 52
Lodge, Henry Cabot, 73
Los Angeles Herald-Express, 170
Los Angeles Times, 4, 39, 80, 88–89,
    95–96, 112, 115, 116, 142, 144, 155,
    159, 162, 166, 186, 196, 197
Lugar, Richard, 108–9
Lynch, Jessica, 161–62

MacArthur, Douglas, 175–76
McBridge, Kelly, 95
McCarthy, Joseph, xvi, 98, 182–83
McClellan, Scott, 54–55, 84, 142
  Thomas's exchanges with, 150–51
McClendon, Sarah, 49, 184–85
McClure's Magazine, 14
McCurry, Michael, 50–51, 82, 90–91
McFarlane, Robert, 21, 22
McGrath, Howard, 16
McGrory, Mary, 185
McMasters, Paul, xix
McNamara, Robert S., 94
Macon Telegraph, 3
Madison Guaranty Savings and Loan, 24
Mann, Fred, 118
Martin, Brian, 93
Martinez, Andres, 116, 117
Mason, Stevens Thomson, 59
Massing, Michael, 143
Mauldin, Bill, 176

Index

ABOUT THE AUTHOR

Helen Thomas is the dean of the White House press corps. She is the recipient of more than thirty honorary degrees and in 1998 was the first recipient of a prize established in her name by the White House Correspondents' Association: the Helen Thomas Lifetime Achievement Award. She is the author of *Dateline: White House, Front Row at the White House,* and *Thanks for the Memories, Mr. President.* She lives in Washington, D.C., where she writes a syndicated column for Hearst.